# The Lean Enterprise

# The Lean Enterprise

*How Corporations Can Innovate Like Startups*

Trevor Owens
Obie Fernandez

WILEY

Cover image: Rayz Ong/Lemongraphic
Cover design: Rayz Ong/Lemongraphic

Published by John Wiley & Sons, Inc., Hoboken, New Jersey.
Published simultaneously in Canada.

The Lean Startup is a trademarked term owned by Eric Ries, along with several other copyrighted and trademarked terms that are used throughout the text. The use of all trademarked or copyrighted terms is by permission of Eric Ries.

For general information on our other products and services or for technical support, please contact our Customer Care Department within the United States at (800) 762-2974, outside the United States at (317) 572-3993 or fax (317) 572-4002.

Wiley publishes in a variety of print and electronic formats and by print-on-demand. Some material included with standard print versions of this book may not be included in e-books or in print-on-demand. If this book refers to media such as a CD or DVD that is not included in the version you purchased, you may download this material at http://booksupport.wiley.com. For more information about Wiley products, visit www.wiley.com.

*Library of Congress Cataloging-in-Publication Data:*

ISBN 978-1-118-85217-0 (Hardcover)
ISBN 978-1-118-85206-4 (ePDF)
ISBN 978-1-118-85218-7 (ePub)

Printed in the United States of America
10 9 8 7 6 5 4 3 2 1

# Contents

# Introduction

Google has a stratospheric market capitalization, but the company that organizes the world's information could easily have been tens of billions of dollars richer. In October 2004, Ev Williams, who had joined the company when it acquired his startup, Blogger, left after a year of chafing under corporate bureaucracy. Blogger product manager Biz Stone departed 11 months later. The pair went on to found Twitter. The new venture went public in November 2013, and was worth $36.7 billion as the new year began.

Losing Williams and Stone was an expensive mistake, but Google didn't learn the lesson. Ben Silbermann joined the company in 2006 after a stint as an IT consultant. He spent nearly two years working on display advertising products but felt out of place as a nonengineer in an engineering-centric culture. He resigned and cofounded Pinterest, the online pinboard service that was valued at $3.8 billion as of January 2014.

Google still didn't get the message, and Kevin Systrom left the company in 2009 after two years of feeling stifled by organizational politics. Not long afterward, he cofounded Instagram, which he sold to Facebook for $1 billion in April 2012.

Williams, Stone, Silbermann, and Systrom—not to mention founders of Asana, Cloudera, Foursquare, Ooyala, and dozens of other young companies—quit because they were unable to exercise their entrepreneurial talents within a large enterprise. We're huge fans of Google. Still, if the iconic Silicon Valley success story, which regularly shows up on lists of the world's most innovative companies, had the potential to keep these brilliant innovators aboard, they left at least $40.5 billion (the combined values of Twitter, Pinterest, and Instagram as of January 2014) on the table.

That's bad news for a paragon of innovation. But it's good news for large, established companies that wish to foster innovation within their own walls. It means that even the most innovative operations are passing up billion-dollar ideas that any enterprise could pick up and run with. It also means that, among the thousands of people working in diverse corporate business units and far-flung offices, there are likely to be scores who have ideas that could create tremendous value. Even the oldest, least savvy companies don't need to repeat Google's mistakes. Enterprises seeking to build new high-growth businesses can unlock and retain latent entrepreneurial talent. They can create an organization that innovates successfully, predictably, and repeatedly—not by chance, but by design.

## Enterprises in Peril

The need for enterprises to innovate has never been more acute. Many established brands are on the ropes. American Airlines was valued at just $5.5 billion at the time it merged with US Airways in 2013. Kodak, a name synonymous with photography for more than a century, retreated into bankruptcy in 2012, with its arch competitor Olympus close behind. Suzuki's automotive division fled the United States the same year, and Volvo appears to be approaching the off ramp. Two cornerstones of the PC industry, HP and Dell (which sold itself for $24 billion in early 2013), are struggling to build a bridge to the post-PC future. BlackBerry's worth has slid to a few billion since it tripped over the very smartphone market it pioneered. Blockbuster has shut down its storefronts and DVD-by-mail services. The death rattles of Radio Shack and JCPenney speak volumes about the challenges in retailing.

This calamity isn't confined to an unfortunate few companies or a particular selection of industries. The threat to established firms is pervasive. Of the names listed in the Fortune 500 in 1955, nearly 87 percent have either gone bankrupt, merged, reverted to private ownership, or lost enough gross revenue to fall off the list. A study of the S&P 500, which ranks companies by market capitalization, found that its constituents averaged 61 years on the list in 1958 but only 18 years in 2012.

Contrast the turmoil in the enterprise world with value creation among the world's most valuable companies as of January 2014. Apple is worth $436.55 billion after three and a half decades in business, a beacon of market-disrupting prowess. Google, less than half that age, is valued at $395.42 billion. Amazon has a market cap of $165.79 billion. Facebook's initial public offering (IPO) was a notorious fiasco, but the 10-year-old company is still worth $164.00 billion and rising. Twitter, founded eight years ago, is already worth $29.60 billion.

Alternatively, consider the fastest-growing companies coming out of the startup crucibles of Silicon Valley and New York. Dropbox, Pinterest, Snapchat, and Uber have accrued valuations approaching $14 billion in a few short years. Newer arrivals such as Airbnb, Evernote, MobileIron, PureStorage, Marketo, Spotify, SurveyMonkey, Violin Memory, and Zscaler are worth more than $1 billion each. In fact, the number of billion-dollar startups is estimated to be as high as 40. These companies are creating value at an unprecedented rate and on a historic scale.

The difference between stagnant enterprises and their fast-growing counterparts is no secret: These emblems of growth have an uncanny ability to bring to market exciting products and services and open vast new markets. High-flying corporations like Amazon and Facebook have proven that big companies can do it. But for lessons in how, the best place to look is startups.

## Startups Ascendant

If the present is a dark time for established companies, it's a golden age for new ventures. Entrepreneurs number 380 million worldwide, according to foundersandfunders.com, a number that's expected to grow exponentially. Superstar entrepreneurs like Steve Jobs and Mark Zuckerberg have become cultural icons, spawning best-selling books and blockbuster movies. *The Social Network*, Hollywood's treatment of the Facebook story, has grossed nearly $300 million worldwide. Hit television show *Shark Tank* features business pitches from aspiring entrepreneurs to a panel of potential investors. The Bravo network even took a chance on a reality TV show, *Start-Ups: Silicon Valley*, which followed a handsome pair of would-be moguls through their efforts to form a business plan and pitch venture capitalists (VCs).

All of which has dulled the appeal of even the biggest enterprise brand names. For bright business- and technology-minded college grads, it's no longer cool to work for a blue-chip corporation. In general, millennials reject the traditional comforts of management hierarchy, financial stability, risk aversion, and buttoned-down culture. They want to work at Airbnb, Dropbox, FourSquare, or Tumblr—or launch their own bid to rule the infosphere.

And, for the first time, it's clear how to do it. Over the past decade, what was a wilderness trail to starting a high-growth business has become a well-worn path. Students can study entrepreneurship in school, read up on the scene in *TechCrunch, VentureBeat,* or *Xconomy,* attend meetups for like-minded aspirants, get a job at a hot startup, draw up a business plan, and start pitching VCs.

More important, the cost of starting a company has fallen through the floor. Many fixed costs have evaporated, replaced by variable costs. For instance, Amazon Web Services gives aspiring entrepreneurs access to data center infrastructure, and it costs nothing until customers start showing up en masse. Freelance communities such as Crowdspring, Mechanical Turk, Odesk, and Elance can handle odd jobs from programming to design to writing press releases. Coworking spaces provide cost-effective offices where startup founders can congregate and support one another until they have sufficient revenue to rent a proper office. Capital has become more accessible as well, thanks to crowdfunding sites such as Kickstarter, seed-funding communities like AngelList, and new laws that allow almost anyone to buy and sell equity.

All these trends boost the level of competition with an enterprise's established business units as well as the possibility that they'll be blindsided by unforeseen market shifts. A new generation of highly empowered entrepreneurs is coming up fast. They have the means, motive, and opportunity to disrupt your business, and they're out to do just that.

## The Enterprise's Dilemma

Hidebound enterprises don't start out that way. As Clayton Christensen pointed out in his classic 1997 business manual, *The Innovator's Dilemma*, most large companies begin as innovators who unseat powerful incumbents by leveraging cheap technology to deliver good-enough capabilities at a lower price. The dilemma arises once they've ascended to dominance. At this point, they have a market to protect, and their original focus on *disruptive innovation* shifts to *sustaining innovation* that bolsters their legacy business. Now exploiting a mature market, they can look forward to decreasing growth. Ultimately, a new competitor emerges that undermines their business with a cheaper alternative. By failing to develop disruptive technologies first, they leave themselves vulnerable.

Indeed, overcoming inertia has become a do-or-die priority for large organizations. Enterprise CEOs must fend off ever more rapid technological shifts and ever more aggressive competitors. Christensen's manual was the first of what has become a flood of books, conferences, workshops, and blogs devoted to the topic, and executives have embraced them in search of a solution. Corporate innovation has become a rallying cry and a budget line item. Intrapreneurship programs have become commonplace. Internal incubators and accelerators are de rigueur. Corporate development funds invest millions in emerging markets. Yet few enterprises escape the innovator's dilemma. Instead, they remain mired in the swamp of inertia, lassitude, bureaucracy, and misaligned incentives that afflict virtually every large company.

The key challenge is resource dependence: the fact that organizations rely on external parties for their survival. Securing these resources implicitly becomes the enterprise's highest priority, regardless of explicit mandates handed down by management. (In the strongest version of this theory, upper-level management has no real control over the company's priorities; external forces determine its direction.) In other words, enterprises aren't free to do what they want. Their suppliers, investors, and especially customers exert a magnetic pull toward established lines of business. This tendency to stay on familiar territory is a strong barrier to innovation.

Overcoming resource dependence is possible but doubtful. Clayton Christensen tells an enlightening story in *The Innovator's Dilemma*. In 1982, Stuart Mabon, CEO of the hard disk manufacturer Micropolis, recognized the need to shift from making 8-inch drives to next-generation 5.25-inch units. Initially he thought he could keep his current customers happy while he made the transition, but he gave up within two years. "It took 100 percent of my time and energy for 18 months," he said, to keep the company dedicated to serving customers for 8-inch drives, as he focused on the new initiative. Ultimately Micropolis made the transition, but Mabon reported the experience to have been the most exhausting and difficult of his life.

We see the influence of resource dependence frequently in our work. Would-be enterprise innovators are staring a substantial opportunity in the face but feel compelled to ask themselves, "How does this fit into our business model? Does it suit our brand? Are we good at it?" These questions are deadly to innovation. The company's values, competencies, and processes are huge advantages in continuing to do what it already does, but they make it nearly impossible to open new territory.

## Unleashing the Enterprise

We've helped numerous enterprises get past these roadblocks. Lean Startup Machine has trained 25,000 entrepreneurs and employees in the Lean Startup method since Trevor Owens founded the company in 2010. Where other trainers teach lean startup methods through lectures and workshops, Lean Startup Machine participants engage hands-on in experimentation, customer development, innovation accounting, and other techniques to bring their business ideas from concept to product, even generating real revenue from real customers. Over an intensive three-day course, participants form hypotheses, test assumptions, interview customers, design products, and validate demand. They leave with practical innovation skills that they can apply immediately.

Working with employees of American Express, Deloitte, ESPN, GE, Google, Intuit, News Corp, Salesforce, Samsung, Time, and thousands of other companies, we've witnessed the obstacles to innovation at large corporations. We've seen the impact of functional silos, quarterly budgeting, salary-based compensation, and corporate politics on entrepreneurial spirit and creative thinking. And we've seen the severe limitations of typical skunkworks, intrapreneur programs, and innovation labs. We've developed an alternative approach that has overcome these challenges, activating latent entrepreneurial talents and skills to transform timid, stodgy organizations into energetic factories of fresh, marketable products and services.

Moreover, we've built a lean startup ourselves. Lean Startup Machine began as a crazy idea born of frustration with previous failed ventures. In three and a half years, it has grown into a worldwide organization that stages 300 boot camps a year in 500 cities, on six continents, funded by Upfront Ventures, Techstars, 500 Startups, and Eric Ries. Now we're developing software that helps innovation teams keep their execution on track. We built Javelin, our software-as-a-service innovation engine, according to the method described in this book, from initial hypothesis through prototype. Since then, we've deployed the tool at scale with Lockheed Martin and News Corp and expect to launch worldwide in early 2014.

We didn't invent the lean startup. Credit for that goes to Eric Ries, Steve Blank, David Kelley, John Krafcik, the 17 writers of the Agile Software Manifesto, and others too numerous to mention. In particular, we owe a huge debt of gratitude to Eric Ries. His book *The Lean Startup: How Today's Entrepreneurs Use Continuous Innovation to Create Radically Successful Businesses* was a landmark achievement. It coalesced Eric's years of research and writings into an easily digestible format that allowed us to take our work to a mainstream business audience, consisting of startups and large companies alike. Notwithstanding, watching many enterprise employees struggle with Lean Startup tenets and practices has led us to extend Eric's work into what we believe is a comprehensive, practical approach that can give established organizations the innovative prowess that's normally thought to be the sole province of startups.

## Why Intrapreneurship Fails

Many enterprise executives try to build an internal culture of innovation. They adorn their offices with ping-pong tables and bowls filled with sugary snacks. They move their best and brightest employees into the role of intrapreneur, an internal entrepreneur accorded the freedom to take risks that ordinarily would be frowned on in the interest of bringing radical new products to market. But most of these efforts come to naught. Intrapreneurs are stymied by politics or sidetracked into low-growth activities. Their most ambitious projects often are wildly misdirected, wasting huge budgets and leaving sterling brands tarnished. Worse, their energy is channeled into slow-moving, me-too products that fail to make a dent in the market. Acquisitions intended to snatch up strategically important technologies or talent suffer from poor integration with the parent company. Bold hires aimed at infusing moribund business units with fresh blood have little effect but to stall promising careers.

In our view, the word intrapreneur is an oxymoron. The *roles of employee and entrepreneur are mutually incompatible.* Executives who expect salaried workers transplanted into an innovation department to come up with great ideas, invest the company's capital in them, and shepherd them to market success are fooling themselves.

Intrapreneurship pro...ams tend to fail for three reasons. First, intrapreneurs are forced to ...dress incremental innovations that lead only to marginal growth. They're not free to focus on high-growth opportunities. Second, they're paid a salary. This removes the motivation that drives real entrepreneurs: the risk of losing everything and the chance of winning a huge payoff. Third, intrapreneurs lack the financial structure to let their projects blossom. Instead, they compete for funding or become mired in departmental backwaters. Let's take a closer look at each of these factors.

### Autonomy

The corporate legacy stifles innovative thinking. Sustaining a mature business demands a tight focus on current customers and existing products. Once employees adopt this mind-set, it's nearly impossible to shake. They internalize the company's values and competencies, which blinds them to potentially industry-changing, high-ROI (return on investment) opportunities that don't fit the established pattern.

Entrepreneurs, on the other hand, think broadly about how to solve customer problems. They spend a lot of time studying the market, playing with products, consulting with other entrepreneurs, sounding out potential customers, and generally looking for ways to get ahead of the market. They need to be located outside the company's offices and given freedom to do whatever is necessary to create an independent business.

## Incentive

Workers don't take big risks without big incentives, which intrapreneurship programs seldom provide. Employees execute well-defined responsibilities in return for agreed-on wages. It's a classic arrangement that satisfies the need for certainty on the part of both employer and employee, but it severely dampens the motivation to dream big and act boldly. The downside of championing a failure far outweighs the upside of creating a success.

Entrepreneurship is about taking big risks in return for the possibility of outsized rewards. This combination of high risk and high reward is immensely motivating. It keeps entrepreneurs going when they encounter seemingly insurmountable obstacles, as they routinely do if they confront market uncertainty head-on. They need to have a personal financial stake in their startups and share in the upside when they succeed, and any enterprise that hopes to benefit from their efforts had better structure their compensation to this effect.

## Financial Structure

Enterprise innovation departments usually have to fight for their budget just like any other business unit. It takes years to build a successful business, so intrapreneurs are likely to have nothing to show on a semi-annual or annual timeline and are forced to play politics. This state of affairs reflects a fundamental misunderstanding of the forces that drive innovation.

Entrepreneurs need a limited runway that keeps them focused and disciplined. At the same time, they need the financial independence to trade equity for funding if they're working on something that shows definite promise even as it's running out of road. Startups don't need to appeal to corporate executives to keep funding a product that might be years away from substantial income. They rely on market forces to confirm their sense of what their startup is worth. Internal innovation efforts require the same constraints and the same freedom.

Most executives who seek to foster an innovative culture fail to recognize that culture is an outgrowth of organizational structure, incentives, and precedents. A culture can't be altered in isolation. Changing culture means changing the organization itself and developing a history around the renewed firm. People are inherently creative and entrepreneurial if they're put in an environment that organizes and incentivizes those qualities.

Until recently, designing such an environment was a tall order. The appropriate structures and processes for innovating in an enterprise context were theoretical, and the theory didn't bear out in real life. Over the past few years, however, the elements have emerged that make it possible to create an enterprise environment in which innovation is not a doomed prospect but an automatic outcome.

## Enter the Lean Startup

Most failed startups die not because they can't build what they set out to build but because customers don't buy it. The fundamental point of the lean startup method is to avoid wasting resources by making products that no one wants.

For instance, a publisher of bike repair manuals aiming to enter the mobile market must choose whether to build products for Android, iOS, Windows Phone, or—dare we say it?—BlackBerry. Which one will its customers want most? It could decide on iOS because that operating system has the largest user base—but perhaps the company's most profitable customers tend to use Android. If the company makes an iOS app and the most profitable customers use Android, the time, expense, and effort of building the product largely will have been wasted.

Successful startups thrive because they have the capacity to learn and adapt to what customers want. Rather than slavishly executing their original plan, they change course based on what they learn and eventually discover a product that customers will pay for and scale it to large numbers of people.

The lean startup method is a set of techniques for accomplishing this product/market validation. If the publisher can determine not only which mobile OS its most profitable customers use, but also whether they would buy a mobile bike manual, through a particular distribution channel, and for what purposes, it can eliminate much of the risk of building the product and create a much higher likelihood of a profitable outcome.

The lean startup movement has proven effective at building viable early-stage ventures at low cost and high speed. Enterprises can adapt lean startup practices to achieve the same results. The discipline of the build-measure-learn loop—iteratively building a minimum viable product, experimenting on real-world customers, and making a decision to pivot or persevere—offers a process of unprecedented efficiency for building sustainable new businesses.

All the arrows in the lean enterprise quiver are essential, but the tactic known as *innovation accounting* is especially relevant to established companies. This technique is the key to driving transformation in old-line companies that ordinarily find innovation beyond their grasp. Let's take a look at how.

## New Tools for CFOs

The constraints that suffocate innovation in an enterprise setting, from resource dependence to issues of autonomy, incentive, and financial independence, are largely tied up in the methods that enterprises use to contain costs. This makes good sense: Data accumulated over a long operating history makes it possible to fine-tune margins and squeeze the highest return on investment out of slow-growing and even contracting markets. However, conventional tools of financial analysis are deadly to innovation. Applying methods designed to deal with predictable economics to situations governed by high uncertainty is counterproductive.

For instance, corporate finance officers are familiar with discounted cash flow (DCF) analysis, a technique that discounts future cash flow based on an interest rate to determine the net present value of a business unit. Early-stage companies lack substantial revenue, and it may be unclear how they may monetize and how their initial revenue strategy may evolve over time. Consequently, DCF isn't appropriate to a startup environment. Instead, early-stage companies are valued based on currently invested capital, demand for equity, and intangible factors that might be characterized as *buzz*. This method is clearly incompatible with what CFOs have been doing for decades.

Innovation accounting is an alternative that makes it possible to measure a startup's progress toward becoming a sustainable business. Conceived by Eric Ries and introduced in his 2011 book, *The Lean Startup*, this technique involves identifying the user behaviors that have the greatest bearing on growth and building a model that reflects their impact on the business. Entrepreneurs can begin tracking startup performance literally on day one by entering into the model fictitious numbers that represent an ideal case. Then, as customers arrive, they can plug in real-world numbers and start tuning the business to generate growth. Moreover, as the product changes, they can add numbers that reflect behaviors around new capabilities to see how they affect the business. The build-measure-learn loop ensures that they validate what they've learned and apply it the next time around.

The metrics model fits well with traditional enterprise practices because it's similar to a DCF. The major difference is that the model is based on user behavior rather than revenue. User behavior may sound like a soft measure compared to cash flow, but for many innovative products, it's the most important. This is because innovative products often require users to adopt a new behavior. Before Facebook, nobody checked their friends' status online; before Twitter, no one wrote public messages in 140 characters. The revenue model for both companies—advertising—is conventional, but the customer behaviors that drive it are unprecedented. If user behavior around this sort of business demonstrates growth, that's the beginning of a viable business.

In this way, innovation accounting allows enterprises to account for the formerly unaccountable. It provides an invaluable tool for enterprise CFOs who need to present the results of innovation efforts to stakeholders. Traditionally, such presentations involve a lot of what Ries calls *success theater*. This method replaces that with accountability and transparency. CFOs can report growth as reflected in the model, and they can propose valuations based on funding levels of early-stage companies of comparable size and focus gleaned from information sources such as AngelList and CrunchBase. This is a powerful way for CEOs to communicate an innovation portfolio's progress and what it means to the company. It provides a rational case for innovation within the enterprise.

## Dawn of the Lean Enterprise

Enterprises are in a tough bind, but our lean enterprise approach offers powerful new tools that can turn companies focused on protecting old markets into masters of discovering and mining new ones.

Innovative companies gain fringe benefits as well. Being perceived as a leader generates a halo effect that can raise the company's public profile and internal morale. This can be a boon to employee retention and recruiting. Establishing an entrepreneurial path within the enterprise attracts not only internal candidates who have ambitions beyond their current job but also outside talent that appreciates the strengths an established company can bring to a new venture; they can live the dream in a more comfortable and stable environment. And developing contacts in the world of startups and seed-stage investors gives the company early warning of emerging trends and business models.

And the impact extends well beyond the company's walls. Today, people who feel an entrepreneurial urge must choose between holding a conventional job and putting their livelihood on the line, subsisting on ramen, and sleeping on the couches of indulgent friends. The lean enterprise offers a third way: They can share the risk with an organization that has been architected to maximize their chance of success. This approach provides a path for would-be entrepreneurs who don't have the means or personality to found a startup on their own, but who may have valuable ideas, talents, and skills. It makes far more efficient use of the entrepreneurial spirit that permeates society at large.

Every company must face the reality that the departure of a single employee can cost the company billions in lost opportunity. There's a better way: Recognize the new rules that govern innovation in this era of pervasive networks, develop a strategy that respects those rules, and build an organization that can execute the strategy in a way that enables the autonomy, incentive, and focus required to innovate. Put entrepreneurs in a special environment that enables the autonomy, incentive, and focus required to innovate. The remainder of this book illuminates the path.

# Chapter 1

# Roadmap

*Introducing the Lean Enterprise*

The root of the enterprise's innovation troubles are the internal failures to address issues of autonomy, incentive, and financial structure. But the overwhelming need to innovate is driven by changes in the outside world. Ubiquitous access to the Internet, mobile networks, and cloud computing re-sculpt the business landscape at ever faster rates. Those forces bring forth new markets and stimulate new products, while building and destroying companies with unsettling speed.

Enterprises need to understand this new environment and its implications for their innovation efforts, and they need to build new structures and strategies that take advantage of these forces rather than being overwhelmed by them. In the chapter entitled Strategy (Chapter 2), we take a closer look at the forces at play and their implications for innovation organizations and strategies.

# The Innovation Colony

Overall, this book explains how to generate a profusion of product or service ideas and figure out which ones are likely to make viable businesses, predictably and repeatedly, within a large organization. The key is a new corporate structure that we call an *innovation colony*. Like the economic and political colonies of previous centuries, an innovation colony is a settlement staffed by employees of the mother company, but it's distant enough that the company's traditional management practices are not in full effect. It's funded by the enterprise, but its main concern is sustaining itself by all possible means, just like a normal startup does. Colonies have single, critical functions to perform on behalf of their enterprise masters: to foster disruptive innovations.

Unlike conventional corporate departments, an innovation colony needs a unique degree of independence and autonomy. It's a company within a company, and it spins out startups at a great rate and fosters the ones that show promise. The chapter entitled Corporate Structure (Chapter 3) covers the colony's organization in detail.

An innovation colony won't produce fresh, market-ready businesses, though, unless the people working in it are properly incentivized. Most entrepreneurs are motivated by a risk/reward profile that would terrify ordinary enterprise employees, and typical compensation structures drive them away. However, in order to succeed, your innovation colony will need people that think like entrepreneurs. The key to hiring them is to create jackpot opportunities. In the chapter entitled Compensation (Chapter 4) we argue that enterprises must be willing to surrender a large share of equity in the ventures they develop. Our rationale is that even if the colony produces a handful of market-leading products, everyone concerned will still make enough money to justify the undertaking.

Innovation colonies pursue large numbers of worthy ideas in alignment with an *innovation thesis* based on prevailing trends in technology, investment, and consumer behavior. We take a closer look at this vision and how to formulate it in Vision: The Innovation Thesis (Chapter 5).

Investing in unproven ideas still entails huge risks. What if none of them hit it big? That risk is the reason why the way you select ideas is as important as the number you pursue. Teams within the innovation colony must test each idea to make sure it has a ready market before committing substantial resources to developing it. The Lean Startup method enables them do exactly that.

## The Lean Startup Method

Fred Wilson, founder of Union Square Ventures, says he likes to invest in startups that "grow like weeds." Why? A weed doesn't need carefully prepared soil, regular watering, or full sunlight. It busts open its seed, sends down roots, and pushes upward without need for a controlled environment. Likewise, ventures built according to lean startup principles don't require the certainty of ideal conditions to thrive. They thrive in conditions of extreme uncertainty—the very conditions that bring the highest returns on investment.

To build a lean enterprise, you must create structures and processes within the company that seek out conditions of high uncertainty, discover promising business possibilities, and nurture the ones that show potential to grow like weeds. Do it right, and you have a shot at harvesting a 10,000-times return.

Doing it right is difficult because corporate people are accustomed to shunning uncertainty. We ended up writing this book because we've been teaching corporations to do lean startup for the past few years, since before Eric's book was even published. In our book, we teach you the step-by-step process to changing your risk-averse corporate mind-set in Lean Enterprise Process (Chapter 6).

Lean startup principles are fundamentally an application of the scientific method—especially experimentation. In conditions of extreme uncertainty, the logical approach is to experiment. Everything we do is pretty much an experiment, but seldom do we apply disciplined procedures to make sure we consistently learn from our experiments. The lean startup method is a framework, complete with terminology, best practices, and a worldwide community of enthusiastic practitioners. It allows you to run experiments at minimum cost while yielding maximum learning. An innovation colony simply aggregates lean startup experiments on a grand scale. It is designed to repeatedly discover innovative new businesses that can generate exponential returns.

## Build, Measure, Learn

In general, the experimental process is an iterative approach divided into three phases: build, measure, and learn. It starts with an inspiration or intuition that customers have a problem and a particular product or service will solve it. The product is never elaborated more than absolutely necessary to complete the current experiment. The point is to build, as quickly and cheaply as possible, an interaction with potential customers that generates measurable results that lead to learning. In this way, you accrue a growing body of real-world knowledge that guides product development, engineering, and marketing efforts. These techniques are the subject of Experimental Methods (Chapter 7).

As you hone your product ideas to appeal to a real-world audience, you need to make sure it can generate a fast-growing business. The lean startup technique known as *innovation accounting* tells you which variables have a decisive impact on factors such as customer acquisition and retention. By building a spreadsheet metrics model of the business and tracking real-world metrics, you can isolate the variables most critical to growth and allocate resources efficiently to optimize them. This is the subject of Innovation Accounting (Chapter 8).

## Product/Market Fit

The ultimate goal of all this experimentation is to achieve product/market fit, the point at which an idea delivers enough value that it can scale quickly to a large customer base. Whether a product or service has achieved product/market fit is largely a subjective judgment. The only proof is an exponentially growing business.

That said, there are two helpful indicators. One is the must-have test. Sean Ellis, the founding head of marketing at Dropbox who is now CEO of Qualaroo, devised this technique while working as a consultant. He used a lightweight tool called *survey.io* to ask a company's customers a single question: "How disappointed would you be if you didn't have access to this product?" After surveying customers of 100 companies, he noticed a pattern. Customers of companies that were struggling to gain traction answered "very disappointed" less than 40 percent of the time. On the other hand, customers of companies that had significant traction answered "very disappointed" at a higher rate. In other words, the company's offering was a must-have for these customers.

---

**Tip**
The must-have indicator can be misleading. For instance, Acceptly, an online service designed to help high school students apply to colleges, garnered a high must-have score, but customers didn't use the site frequently enough to make a sustainable business. In such a situation, trying to scale up can be challenging. You can use further survey questions to test for flaws like this.

---

The other indicator of product/market fit comes from the innovation accounting. An important part of building a metrics model is to enter a set of fictional measures that represent a successful business. When the real-world metrics match or exceed this ideal case, it's a good sign that the business has reached product/market fit.

## Three Strategies

The lean startup techniques of experimentation and innovation accounting form the basis for three strategies designed to enable enterprises to create groundbreaking new products. The first is to incubate internally. This is the subject of Incubate Internally (Chapter 9).

Occasionally, a compelling idea will be already in development by an independent startup. The second strategy then comes into play: acquire early. A well-timed acquisition can bring valuable resources into the enterprise and jumpstart innovation efforts that can continue alongside internal startups. In Acquire Early (Chapter 10) we take a look at how to accomplish this.

The third strategy is to invest in outside startups. There are several reasons to do this. A startup may be too risky to acquire or simply may not be up for sale. In situations like this, an enterprise can purchase a stake that may have enormous upside potential without having to make the commitment of incubating or acquiring. Investing is the subject of Invest When You Can't Acquire (Chapter 11).

Some enterprises won't want to dive head-first into the waters of high risk and high reward, preferring to wade into the depths in small steps. But even a small innovation colony can vet enough ideas to generate a hit. The chapter entitled Innovation Flow (Chapter 12) explains how to scale a colony from a limited trial run to a massive operation.

These structures, methods, techniques, and strategies add up to a powerful toolkit that's available to any enterprise with the ambition and commitment to take destiny into its own hands. There's no need to lumber along in a rut of *sustaining innovation*. The path to breakthrough products and exponential growth is wide open. Enterprises can compete with startups on their own turf—and win. Let's see how.

---

### Case Study: GE, Stephen Liguori, Executive Director, Global Innovation

General Electric (GE) ranked ninth on *Bloomberg Businessweek's* 2013 list of the world's most innovative companies. Not bad for a business that rated number eight in the same year's Fortune 500 list of the world's largest enterprises—and positively astounding for a company that was founded in 1892 and now boasts more than 300,000 employees and nearly $150 billion in revenue (fiscal 2012). Much of the credit goes to their CEO Jeff Immelt and GE leaders such as Stephen Liguori. As GE's executive director of global innovation, Liguori and a dedicated team are pioneering the use of lean startup techniques in the arena of industrial hardware. His FastWorks program was developed through working with Eric Ries and is driving lean startup practices throughout the company to stimulate breakthrough products and open new markets. Liguori and his colleagues are solving the most intractable challenges of enterprise innovation through bold leadership. He spoke with us about the path he's taking to get there.

#### How Are Your Innovation Efforts Structured? Do You Have a Special Innovation Division?

We don't have a special division. There are two halves to the innovation equation at GE. The first is technical innovation, inventing new machines. We have seven Global Research centers worldwide, including a new one with 700 software engineers in Silicon Valley, who work with every GE division. The other half is commercial innovation. Beth Comstock, our CMO, heads a small hit squad doing that. I'm the executive director for global innovation. Sue Segal is president of GE Ventures, and there's a licensing team that looks for ways to take advantage of the thousands of patents we have.

### *How Do You Keep Innovation Efforts Free of Interdepartmental Politics, Budgeting Cycles, and Other Corporate Roadblocks?*

It's the heart of the issue. When you combine the bureaucracy that builds up in a large organization with the highly technical nature of the things we make—jet engines, power turbines, CAT scan machines—you could say it's daunting. Our solution is FastWorks, a program built on lean startup principles. If you don't recognize that the culture is the enemy, you'll lose. You've got to go top and bottom. At the top, you have to get not only sponsorship but also buy-in and understanding. We're putting executives through training in lean startup principles, telling them, "You have to know how to do it because if you're not going to change your behavior"—that's literally what we're talking about—"we'll die." The flip side is giving the teams tools and training. They say, "I want to be an entrepreneur, but I get choked to death by the functions. The finance guys say prove it, the legal guys say it's too risky, the compliance guy says the regulatory people will have problems with it."

### *How Would You Answer Them?*

One of the ways you get the buy-in with the bureaucracy and the culture is by telling everyone, "We're not betting the ranch." We're not going to build a factory to roll out thousands

*(Continued)*

*(Continued)*

or millions of new, innovative machines. We might make a million refrigerators a year, but we're making only 60 of the conceptually disruptive refrigerator we've been working on. It's not the old, "Give it to engineering and come back three years later"—and, in our case, $30 million later. It's like, "How about we give you $30,000 and 30 days and you come back with a prototype." Then the engineers say, "Do you know how much money it will cost me to set up to make a prototype? My yield will go down, my waste will go up, my metrics will go in the toilet and I'll get screwed at my annual review." It's not that the incentives are set up wrong; they're set up great for running the mother ship. This is not the mother ship. We're telling the teams that the "minimum" in a minimum viable product is not just in terms of the features; it's also the smallest number of customers who need to use it to get real learning. You might make five prototypes of a locomotive and give one to each of the big north American railroads—just 1, not 50, not 500, not 5,000—and that contains the risk to the system. We're doing it to discover a need in the marketplace, not to scale yet, not to make money yet. That opens the window to get people to listen to these radically different ideas. "We don't know if it's a big idea yet, so we're not looking to blow up the world. We just are looking to do a small test."

### How Do You Think About Staffing for Innovation?

There are only five on Beth's team. A senior group of execs asked us just the other day, "Do you need more people to do this?" We said, "No." It's probably the first time at a GE meeting where someone was offered more resources and said no! There are two reasons why we did that. First, there's not a startup in the world where they don't talk about the scarcity of resources. We've learned that it's not about how many resources you have; it's about having the right focus. Second, if this becomes a mandate from headquarters, it will fail. We're spreading the word, GE division by GE division. There's a team from GE's energy business, they make unbelievably huge, complicated generators that go in power plants, plus every piece of what's called *transmission and distribution*. It's just mind-bogglingly complicated. They want to try FastWorks on three new product ventures to get into a radically new space. Here's the punch line: They'll staff it and fund it. I'll bring in an entrepreneur who can coach them in how to be startup-like in GE. We want buy-in by the teams: "You put your skin in the game. You put your people and money in to fund it. We'll provide the training and coaching and tools to help you do it."

### Would It Be Productive to Structure Compensation Like a Typical Startup, in Which Founders Give Up as Much as Half Their Salary in Return for Equity in the Projects They Develop?

The compensation plans today do not include equity, but we'd love to get into that. I did a Google hangout with a couple of folks on crowdsourcing. We literally crowdsourced some jet engine parts, believe it or not. The guy who won was from Indonesia. Second place was from Hungary, and third place was from Poland. It's amazing the smart people you can find around the globe. The question came up, "How much are you paying this person?" We paid the winner $7,000. Someone said, "Couldn't GE potentially make millions of dollars from that?" Yes, we could. So we're trying to figure out the right incentive system for internal startups as well as for crowdsourcing.

Here are the counterpoints: When you're a startup within GE, you have resources and career stability, but if we don't provide the right rewards, they'll leave. So we're aware that we need to let employees put some compensation at risk so they can have a much bigger payout. I'll tell you a hysterical story.

*(Continued)*

(*Continued*)

Our head of HR sat down with a group of relatively senior managers and said, "We want to start doing this lean startup thing and we want to incent GE teams. If we're going to ask them to do this, we have to give them the offset of big bonuses or equity stakes in what they're developing." This is the head of HR! Amazing! The managers said, "Are you crazy?" The very people who say, "I need more innovators and risk takers" are worried about screwing up the compensation system. Will we go all the way to equity or spinning off joint ventures? I can't answer that question today, but I can guarantee that we'll be experimenting in the next year or so.

### Is There a Vision or a Thesis That Directs or Places Boundaries Around Innovation Efforts?

We probably have two theses. One is to move from building business models on equipment to building them on holistic systems and solutions. How about, instead of providing airlines with jet engines, we provide power by the hour. We say to a power plant, "We'll tie in wind farms and solar farms, and the more power we give you, the more you'll pay us because it lowers your operating costs." That kind of business is very different for a company that grew up building and selling physical pieces of machinery. The other is that the world is becoming increasingly connected and increasingly kinetic—from a speed standpoint—and we'll either innovate faster or be disrupted. It's an opportunity to tap our domain knowledge and heritage around technology and do even smarter things with it. We've got to move with market speed or market intensity.

### What Role Does the Lean Startup Method Play in FastWorks?

The lean startup method is absolutely one of the key pieces. Jeff Immelt's annual letter to investors for 2013, said that two of the best books he had read lately are *The Lean Startup* by Eric Ries and *The Startup Playbook* by David Kidder. Those are the only two books he mentioned in a five-page letter, which speaks to the fact that the lean startup method is one of the core influences on what we're trying to do. Every company needs to figure out how it applies to them. We take the principles and morph them to make sense for us.

### *How Do You Use Metrics? Do You Use Innovation Accounting to Track the Progress of Projects Before They Earn Substantial Revenue?*

We're beginning to. Right now, we're actively working with a dozen or so projects where the goal is to identify metrics and develop innovation accounting techniques.

### *How Do You Know When One of Your Projects Has Reached Product/Market Fit?*

We know we've reached product/market fit when the market leaders, the early adopters, say, "I'm in." That's not as subjective as it might sound. We're encouraging people to come up with 10-times-better solutions: Don't just be marginally better than the competition, make it 10 times better. If you're 10 times better, the customer will say, "I've got to have that." Then we know we've got something. We've got software that lets hospitals run better; think of it as air traffic control for hospitals. If you put that software in a hospital for a 90-day trial and at the end of 90 days they say, "Don't take that software out," we know it has reached product/market fit.

### *What Percentage of Your Projects Is Incubated Internally, versus Acquisitions and Investments?*

For us, a bolt-on acquisition is $2 billion to $4 billion, and we'll continue to do those. We also do investments with people

*(Continued)*

(*Continued*)

who can act as partners who get us up the curve quicker. We put $100 million into Pivotal, the VMWare spinoff, and $30 million into Quirky, the consumer appliance startup. The pendulum is swinging toward finding things earlier, inventing them ourselves, and finding partners who synergize with what we're doing. Look at what we've done with our Silicon Valley Global Research Center. Those 700 software engineers are there fundamentally for organic growth on the industrial Internet. If you go back 10 years ago, GE grew predominately by acquisition. We're much more balanced now.

### What's the Percentage of Acquisitions versus Acqui-Hires?

We're in the early stages of looking at acqui-hires. We've done a couple of small acqui-hires to date, and I expect you'll see more of that.

### How Can You Scale Innovation Efforts?

GE is unique in its physical scale. It's partly a matter of training at three levels: executives, coaches, and rank and file. External experts are helping us train a couple of coaches per GE business. We're up to 80 or 100 coaches who train people on real projects with real GE businesses. Our goal is to scale that as rapidly as we can, but keep the quality going.

### Case Study: Intuit, Hugh Molotsi, Vice President, Intuit Labs Incubator

Intuit is a legend among Silicon Valley legends. Founded at the dawn of the PC revolution by Scott Cook and Tom Proulx, the company fended off competitors including Microsoft to become the dominant maker of software for personal finance and small business accounting. Intuit was an early adopter of principles later incorporated into the lean startup method, so by the time the lean startup movement reached full flower in 2011, the company—by then a full-scale international enterprise—embraced it wholeheartedly. Hugh Molotsi joined in 1993 as a software engineer and eventually took on leadership of innovation. As vice president of Intuit Labs, he's responsible for encouraging and supporting innovation throughout the company, which employs 8,500 people and generated $4.15 billion in revenue during fiscal 2012. He blogs at blog.hughmolotsi.com.

### How Do You Structure Your Innovation Activities? Do You Have a Special Innovation Division?

One of the things that makes us different from many companies is that we consider innovation everyone's job. There's no set of people who figure out what we're going to be doing in the future. Good ideas come from everywhere, and frontline employees who are interacting with customers are more likely than executives to have the key insights that we need to come up with new ideas.

### How Do You Manage Innovation Without a Structure?

Well, it's literally unstructured. Every Intuit employee gets 10 percent of their time to work on ideas they think will drive growth. We call that unstructured time. We don't track it; we just put it out there as an aspirational goal and let people decide for themselves how to spend it. We teach everyone two core capabilities: customer-driven innovation and Design for Delight, which is our version of design thinking. So people spend time at their discretion coming up with ideas and moving them forward.

*(Continued)*

(*Continued*)

### How Do Employees Get Resources They Need to Develop Their Ideas?

Once you have an idea, the main challenge is to get it into customers' hands. We created Intuit Labs as a sort of service organization that helps employees run experiments and develop products without needing management input, support, or resources. There are about a dozen of us. Our epiphany was that unstructured-time teams are startups, and they frequently run into similar kinds of challenges. We're trying to make it easier for them and turn ideas into minimum viable products that they use to run experiments with customers. Some people need an iOS programmer, designer, web host, payment processing. We try to eliminate those problems. Or they can sign up for an Incubation Week, which is a week of intensive coaching from other developers and designers with the goal of releasing something to the public by the end of the week. Once they've built an MVP, they can use the Intuit Labs website to acquire their first customers.

### Does Intuit Labs Have a Physical Location?

No, it's more a conceptual notion. It's a friendly place for innovation teams that grow out of unstructured time projects and aren't getting the support they need from management.

### How Do You Keep Innovation Efforts Free of Interdepartmental Politics, Budgeting Cycles, and Other Roadblocks That Typically Hamper Enterprise Innovation?

That's hard. We run into it all the time. My short answer is, unstructured time is free of all that by definition, because employees are free to use it as they see fit. If someone wanted to develop a Windows Mobile application, their manager might say, "Windows Mobile isn't one of our strategic mobile platforms," but that wouldn't stop the person because that person has full prerogative over how to use that time. That's a big way we unbuckle ourselves not only from legacy applications but from what might prove, over time, to be an ill-conceived strategy. A few years ago, our big mobile platforms were Windows and BlackBerry. Fast-forward and it's all about Android and iPhone. We're constantly making decisions about what we're going to focus on, but they change very quickly. Sometimes, in hindsight, we realize that it wasn't the right strategy. The beauty of unstructured time is that we're not hindered by that strategy. If somebody has passion, they can go for it, and if it works, it can grow into a major line of business.

### How Is the Staff Compensated? Would It Be Productive to Structure Compensation Like a Typical Startup, in Which Founders Give Up as Much as Half Their Salary in Return for Equity in the Projects They Develop?

We don't do anything special. When people work on unstructured time, their motivation is less about becoming wealthy than the sense of accomplishment and pride in improving customers' financial lives. People who do well at innovation are rewarded in the normal ways that we manage performance and provide compensation. For instance, somebody who is a product manager probably would get promoted. Having said that, every year, we recognized employees for having delivered real benefits in their work around innovation. The Scott Cook Innovation Award is a company-wide recognition. The award recognizes employees whose innovations have created significant value for Intuit employees, customers, or shareholders. Winners also get three months of full-time or six months of half-time to work on whatever they want, because innovators have asked for more time to follow their passions. They

*(Continued)*

(*Continued*)

also get a vacation anywhere they want to go for themselves and a significant other. In addition, we also have the Founder's Innovation Award for outstanding achievement in innovation. I'm generally shy about bringing this up because I'm the only person who has won it so far. But I received the cash and stock equivalent of $1M in 2011 for helping create our Payments business. So Intuit employees also have this award to look forward to if their venture turns into a big success.

### Do You Worry That Entrepreneurially Minded People Will Leave?

Absolutely. In our Rotational Development Program, we look for people who have just graduated from college and have high leadership attributes and entrepreneurial capabilities. They tend to have a great impact when they come to Intuit. But like with most millennials, long-term retention is a challenge and many leave after a few years. They say, "I have this idea. I'd rather work in a small company or start something myself." At the end of the day, there are pros and cons to taking that risk with a small company. The ones who have stayed for longer careers find Intuit compelling as a growing company with lots of opportunity to drive your own projects.

### How Do You Choose Which Projects to Support? How Do You Prioritize?

That's a problem we look forward to having. We look for who's most ready to build an MVP. Sometimes it's very clear what a team aims to build and the issue is having time or support to do it. Those teams are perfect for us to help. On the other hand, we can usually see when someone has an idea that hasn't really been thought through. Sometimes we recommended that they sign up for LeanStartIN, a two-day internal event where they get help designing their business model and running lean experiments that don't involve coding. At the end of that experience, they're usually in a much better place to know what they want to build and test. More than 100 teams have gone through it, and they've been successful to the tune of generating $20 million in new revenue in eight months.

### How Do Projects Get Funded?

We help the teams get to a point where they have a compelling story that they can pitch to a business unit for funding. On rare occasions, we see something that looks like it could be a big strategic business for the company, but it doesn't align with any of our existing business units. We don't want to lose the idea just because it doesn't fit into our current company structure. In those cases, we may end up funding and incubating it as an Intuit Labs project. Brainstorm is a great example. It's a collaborative idea generation tool that began as an unstructured-time project, and we use it internally. A few years ago, we decided to try to sell it to other companies. It's a small business. It doesn't fit any of the business units we have today, but we feel like it could be a good business for Intuit.

### What Role Does the Lean Startup Method Play in All This?

We're applying the lean startup across the board in terms of how we build products. We used to have this debate: Do you figure out all the requirements up front, come up with the perfect plan, the right architecture, and then you build it? Or do you get ideas into customers' hands and experiment? That's no longer a debate. Lean experimentation is the approach we use.

### Do You Use Innovation Accounting to Track the Progress of Projects Before They Earn Substantial Revenue?

We have nascent thoughts about how to use innovation accounting. The lean startup method has had the biggest impact on our approach to developing new applications. We

*(Continued)*

(*Continued*)

do rapid experimentation, we value data over opinions, and we look for efficient ways to get that data.

### How Do You Know When One of Your Projects Has Reached Product / Market Fit?

Right now, it's very qualitative. During the month after SparkRent first went out, the team got a couple dozen landlords to sign up, so they were confident they had a good fit early on. On the other hand, BizRecipes has been out for a couple of months, and we've got some good traffic, but I don't think the team or anyone else feels like we've nailed product/ market fit. As we mature, I suspect that we'll get much more rigorous in how we make that decision.

### Do You Integrate Oversight of Incubation, Acquisition, and Strategic Investment, or Are They Handled Separately?

Right now they're separate, but we've been talking about integrating them. Historically, we've been able to move really fast in partnership with outside entities, and a partnership can become an acquisition later. We'd like to make partnerships an element of how we help internal startups move faster. How can we make it easy for an internal startup team to work with an external entity to design a test, run the test, and decide whether we want to do something more formal with that entity? That's not my focus this year, but I'm thinking about it for the future.

### How Do You Scale Innovation Efforts?

Our goal is to get half of our employees to use unstructured time, so half are doing some sort of exploration. That translates into quite a lot of activity. Scaling up is about teaching people about the tools and techniques. Then, hopefully, they can incorporate those things not just into their unstructured-time projects but into their day job as well.

# Chapter 2

# Strategy

The environment for innovation has evolved dramatically in recent years. Not long ago, raising capital was difficult, determining what people would buy was hit-or-miss, developing new products was slow and cumbersome, and attracting large numbers of customers was costly. These barriers have fallen as, in the memorable phrase of venture capital superstar Marc Andreessen, "software is eating the world."

In an essay published in the *Wall Street Journal* in August 2011, Andreessen called attention to the fact that an increasing variety of products and services were being delivered in the form of digital code. A decade after the dot-com bubble burst, he noted, the infrastructure was finally in place to distribute software directly to businesses and consumers, via the Internet, to laptops, phones, tablets, and a growing variety of so-called smart consumer devices such as ereaders, wristwatches, and media players.

The book industry is a clear example. Bibliophiles once flocked to Barnes & Noble to buy the latest best sellers. Now they download them from Amazon.com and view them on their Kindles—no more printing, no more driving, no more brick-and-mortar stores. The same scenario is playing out in all the publishing industries—newspapers, magazines, maps, music, movies, games—but it doesn't stop there. Facebook and Google Plus hangouts are replacing face-to-face social events. Coursera, Khan Academy, and Udacity are replacing schools. Photography has become a digital pastime, a feature of phones and online storage services. Telephony itself has been encroached by Skype, FaceTime, and Google Voice. With the rapid advances and falling cost of 3-D printing, it may not be far-fetched to think that our children will download and print household items rather than picking them up from local retailers or ordering them online.

The ascendency of software delivered through increasingly ubiquitous mobile, cloud, and social networks fundamentally changes the landscape for entrepreneurs. The old rules no longer apply. Any innovation strategy needs to take into account five principles of this new environment:

1. Market shifts are unpredictable.
2. Small teams create immense value.
3. New markets are winner-take-all.
4. Speed is the only competitive advantage.
5. For every success, there are a multitude of failures.

These are the rules that now govern the innovation game. Let's take a closer look at them.

### Market Shifts Are Unpredictable

Clayton Christensen was the first to say that the marketable use of disruptive innovations is unknowable at the time they're invented. Today this is truer than ever. New platforms, especially, can cause markets to change in unpredictable ways.

Christensen drew a clear line between sustaining and disruptive innovation, but those distinctions are no longer sufficient. Many new products fall into neither category and might be characterized as *rippling innovation*. Coined by Brandt Cooper, one of our good friends in the Lean Startup world, this phrase describes developments built on products and services that serve as platforms for *open development*.

Twitter, for example, created a new kind of communication network that has changed the way people use previous networks such as e-mail, text messaging, the web, and telephony. But the company also provides access to its infrastructure through an application programming interface (API). Dozens of companies have taken advantage of the Twitter API to create independent businesses such as HootSuite, SocialFlow, and Topsy. These parasitic companies use Twitter for their own ends. They're not necessarily trying to disrupt other communication channels, steal Twitter's customers, or compete with one another; in fact, many have nothing in common beyond their use of the Twitter API.

In this way, the Twitter platform unleashes "open" market forces that are difficult to assess and whose outcomes are impossible to foretell. Twitter is just one of thousands of companies that offer API resources. The list includes heavyweights such as Amazon, eBay, Facebook, and Google, plus countless smaller players. Any of those APIs can spawn innovations that *ripple* into unpredictable new markets. Immense opportunities can open up when and where you least expect them.

Given the unpredictability of these market trends, the only sensible approach is to embrace uncertainty and build your strategy around it. Your efforts must be geared toward relentless experimentation so that you can discover opportunities as soon as they emerge. Your corporation must have access to a large pool of ideas and be flexible enough to participate in new ventures in any way possible. The corporation must be ready to pull the plug immediately on projects that indicate negligible market potential. A corporate innovation manager's job isn't to pick winners; it's to create opportunities for winners to rise above the chaos.

Sound familiar? Actually it shouldn't, because it's the opposite of how most enterprises function. But let's get back to those four principles, the second of which is. . . .

### Small Teams Create Enormous Value

Creating products and bringing them to market once required huge teams and heavyweight support infrastructure. Not anymore. Today, small groups can create outsized value and change the course of markets; think of AngelList (50 employees worth $150 million) or Snapchat (21 employees valued at at least $800 million, and they recently turned down a $3 billion offer). In many situations, small teams are more effective than large ones.

In our previous lives as software consultants, we've constantly told hiring managers to hire half or less of the headcount they were planning, but to spend the same on salaries. The fact is that small, highly skilled teams move faster, and are more flexible and responsive to market conditions. A small team can build a simple product, distribute it to a global customer base, and create millions of dollars of value in a matter of months.

Efficiencies driven by new technology are empowering even single individuals to coordinate and achieve results that formerly required entire corporate departments. Building software takes fewer engineers thanks to advanced software development frameworks such as Ruby on Rails.

Our friends Tom Preston-Warner, PJ Hyett, and Chris Wanstrath founded Github, which is the dominant global repository of open-source building blocks for software. They launched it in 2008 as a side project using Ruby on Rails. At a year old, Github reached 100,000 users. A year later, with only a few more hires, they announced that they were hosting more than a million code repositories. And in July 2012, still employing less than 100 people, and boasting impressive and steady revenue growth, Github announced an unprecedented (and unneeded) $100M Series A round that valued the four-year-old company at a whopping $750M. The hotly contested round was led by Andreessen Horowitz, who called it their largest single investment ever.

Sysadmins and IT staff seem like ancient history when cloud computing resources like Amazon Web Services let ordinary programmers tap limitless arrays of server racks and hard disks like on command, just like magic. There's no need for a huge marketing department when you can promote your product virally using Facebook and Twitter, and no need for distribution managers when you can sell product through the App Store, Amazon, eBay, or Shopify. The number of manufacturing personnel required to produce hard goods is dramatically reduced by contract manufacturing services and prototyping is drastically simplified by the emergence of 3-D printing.

Older companies haven't yet internalized this stuff we're talking about. As recently as 2011, News Corp hired 100 employees and spent $30 million to build the world's first iPad-only news app, called the Daily. The project made a brief PR-driven splash, only to be shut down a year later. During the same time period, journalists Jim Giles and Bobbie Johnson cofounded Matter, a magazine for the web and iPad. They raised $140,000 on Kickstarter and hired a staff of five, and sold the company the following year for an undisclosed sum to Twitter cofounder Ev Williams, who folded it into his own new publishing startup called Medium.com.

Instagram had only 13 employees when it was acquired by Facebook for $1 billion. Mailbox, likewise, had a team of 13 when Dropbox acquired it for around $100 million. Some entrepreneurs create similar results single-handedly. Swedish developer Marcus Persson built Minecraft, a phenomenally popular computer game that has sold nearly 13 million copies at $26.95 each. Andrey Ternovsky, a 17-year-old high school student in Moscow, coded Chatroulette, which quickly became the premier app for video chat. The list goes on and on.

One effect is to boost competition. In the past, you might employ a team of 50 to fend off one competitor. Now that teams can get just as much done with five people, there are enough skilled workers to staff 10 competitors. By the same token, though, the dramatic drop in the price of starting competitive companies gives you the opportunity to build large numbers of startups on a limited budget.

The growing ability of small teams to create value gives corporate innovators an incentive to organize their operations around groups of only two or three people. There's no need to spend large amounts of capital on an extensive staff and operations. A bunch of tiny teams, supplemented by contract resources, can multiply the enterprise's power to generate ideas, validate them, and develop them into marketable products and services.

## New Markets Are Winner-Take-All

Despite proliferating competition, only one company will dominate emerging market niches. There are no serious competitors to Amazon, eBay, Facebook, Google, LinkedIn, Netflix, Twitter, Uber, YouTube, Wikipedia, and a host of other Internet leaders. The same is increasingly true in hardware products that connect to networks, such as Fitbit, iPad, Kindle, Nest, and Pebble.

In a connected world, huge advantages accrue to players that take full advantage of network effects (known to economists as demand-side economies of scale). The value of a network is the square of the number of network nodes, according to Metcalfe's Law, attributed to 3Com founder Robert Metcalfe. That value rises exponentially with the number of nodes. The canonical example is the telephone, which becomes more useful as more people have one. Online social networks exhibit the same property: The more people use eBay, Facebook, or LinkedIn, the more useful those services become, and the harder it is for competitors to horn in on their action. As network connections become crucial to a broader array of products—cars connected via OnStar, headphones connected via Bluetooth, heart rate monitors connected to medical and insurance networks, thermostats connected to power generators, and so on—they, too, become subject to network effects.

Large, established companies tend to think they can win markets by acquiring also-ran competitors or starting their own and then leveraging their strength in branding, marketing, and distribution. The days when this strategy could work are long past. Case in point: Craigslist. The top classified-ad site is notoriously user-unfriendly and archaic. Many companies have tried to unseat it, but no one has. Why? Because Craigslist is the acknowledged leader in classified advertising. Its existing user base generates an unstoppable positive feedback loop: All the buyers are there, so all the sellers are there, ad infinitum.

Networked information is subject to a similar dynamic known as the superstar effect. Disproportionate rewards accrue to the acknowledged leader in any field, be it entertainment, sports, politics, technology, or retailing. This phenomenon makes the top name in any given category a magnet not only for audiences but for funding, talent, and other essential resources. "Small differences in talent at the top of the distribution will translate into large differences in revenue," economist Sherwin Rosen writes.

The explanation for this phenomenon is surprisingly simple. Where distribution is limited, the audience has little choice but to take what it can get. However, the Internet makes all players equally accessible, and there's no reason to settle for second best. Number one is the rational choice. The Internet creates superstar markets, and that gives you opportunity to seize the initiative in emerging niches. If you occupy the top slot, competitors will have a hard time ousting you.

The fact that new markets are winner-take-all liberates corporate innovators from the pressure to imitate competitors and reproduce the flavor of the month. It gives them license—rather, a mandate—to disconnect from the corporate brand and produce something genuinely new and potentially disruptive. The only option is to get ahead of the market and reach early adopters with something that solves novel, unrecognized problems. Innovation efforts must be structured to recognize such opportunities and sharpen their offerings to take maximum advantage of them.

### Speed Is the Only Competitive Advantage

The surest way to become number one is to reach the market ahead of competitors. In *The Innovator's Dilemma*, Christensen noted that the only companies to gain substantial market share in the hard disk drive industry were those that launched a product within the first two years after the technology became available. The window of opportunity has only become narrower since he wrote the book in 1997.

This perspective contradicts the conventional business-school wisdom that pioneers end up with arrows in their backs. Historically, companies that were first to market with a given product or service typically fell into the chasm that separates early adopters from the early majority, to adopt the metaphor proposed by Geoffrey Moore in his classic marketing guidebook, *Crossing the Chasm*. Imitators who followed could benefit from the first mover's mistakes and successfully address mainstream customers. This is no longer true. Today, the first to market nearly always wins.

First-mover advantage is driven by a potent force. The pace of technological change is increasing exponentially, futurist Ray Kurzweil observed. In practical terms, this means that technology will change while new products are in development, and by the time customers are ready to buy them, there may well be something new following very close behind. At the same time, distribution channels are becoming increasingly efficient. The amount of time it takes for products to attract a critical mass of customers is shrinking. The telephone took 75 years to reach 50 million users. Radio took 38 years, television 15, Facebook 3.5. Angry Birds took only 35 days. In such circumstances, speed is the only real advantage there is.

Being first confers three powerful benefits. First, you can learn what customers want and how to give it to them. Anyone who comes after you must climb the same learning curve. This sounds simple, but the challenges can be subtle, especially in the design of user interfaces, where the way you expose basic features can make a tremendous difference in user adoption and retention. Second, you gain access to early adopters. These users are your toehold in the market, what we call in Lean Startup world, "early evangelists," because they exert a crucial influence over the early majority (not to mention press, investors, and talent) that will carry your product into the mainstream. If you can gain their trust and loyalty, competitors will have to work harder to attract them. Finally, when you're first to market, all channels of distribution are wide open. The press will mention your launch, social network users will distribute links, and search advertising will be at its least expensive. For latecomers, these channels are more costly and less effective.

Consider Facebook's attempts to copy popular apps. Facebook built Places to replicate Foursquare, Messenger to replace WhatsApp, Poke to overshadow Snapchat. They were all released within months of the originals, yet they failed because their capabilities didn't outweigh the hassle of switching. The effect is even more intense when it involves hardware products like Microsoft's Zune. The early adopters had already latched onto the iPod when Zune came along, and the Zune itself provided little reason to switch. The press labeled it a me-too product and the buzz fizzled. It left barely a ripple as it sank. History repeated itself as Microsoft Surface failed to make an impression against massive sales of Apple's iPad.

If corporate innovators must wait for funding, approval, or attention from specialized departments, they'll be fighting with both hands tied behind their back. You must empower them to do anything necessary to continue learning what customers want until they have it. This is a bitter pill for many enterprises to swallow. *What about protecting the brand? What about shielding profitable departments? What about insulating customers from irritating engineers? What about making quarterly numbers?* None of these concerns outweigh the need for speed when the fate of the company as a whole hangs in the balance.

### For Each Success, There May Be a Thousand Failures

Everyone knows that building a startup, or investing in one, isn't a sure bet. But even the most experienced early-stage investors have a hard time wrapping their heads around the mind-boggling degree of uncertainty that governs returns on a new venture. A vanishingly small number of early-stage investments will pay off 10,000 times. A few will pay off 10 times. The vast majority will lose every penny invested. If there's a way to distinguish one from another ahead of time, Silicon Valley's savviest investors haven't discovered it.

In technical terms, startup investment returns follow a power law. The most valuable startup in the portfolio of the Y Combinator accelerator, Dropbox, was worth $10 billion as of January 2014. That's more than all the other Y Combinator companies combined, which total $14.4 billion. The second most valuable, Airbnb, is worth $2.5 billion, more than the combined value of every one listed below it, which comes to $1.4 billion. And so on. To view it another way, Y Combinator would be worth less than half as much if a single company were missing from its roster.

Similarly, a venture capital (VC) firm will invest in 10 companies hoping that one will pay off 10 times or 100 times. That one win covers the losses incurred by the other nine, which are considered a cost of doing business. The earlier in the life of a company you buy in, the greater the potential upside. In early-stage investing, you might invest in thousands of companies to find one that pays off 10,000 times.

An interesting upshot of this phenomenon is that the best investments initially look like bad ideas. This makes a certain amount of common sense: If an idea looks good, big companies likely are already working on it. Therefore, you need to take chances on ideas that aren't so obvious. Peter Thiel, cofounder of Paypal and Palantir, draws a Venn diagram of the overlap between two circles. Once circle represents ideas that look bad. The other represents ideas that pay off big. Billion-dollar opportunities, he says, are found in the tiny area of overlap.

There's plenty of evidence to support Thiel's observation. In 1876, Western Union declined to purchase Alexander Graham Bell's telephone patent for only $100,000, according to a well-worn business-school parable. More recently, Andreessen Horowitz's partner Chris Dixon pointed to Airbnb, Dropbox, eBay, Google, and Kickstarter as companies that struck him initially as highly unlikely to make money. Even Y Combination's founder Paul Graham isn't immune. "One of my most valuable memories is how lame Facebook sounded to me when I first heard about it," Graham writes in a blog post. "A site for college students to waste time? It seemed the perfect bad idea: a site (1) for a niche market (2) with no money (3) to do something that didn't matter." It's a good bet that he regrets missing out on an opportunity that was valued at $155 billion as of January 2014.

The message is clear. If you're innovating products and services from scratch, expect to try a ton of ideas, many of them counterintuitive, before you find one that actually works. VCs talk about deal flow, a way of describing their access to potential deals. Corporate innovation efforts need to generate immense *innovation flow*, or access to ideas that might spawn billion-dollar businesses. You need to access a pool of literally thousands of ideas over the course of a few years with the aim of developing the most promising among them to product/market fit.

This is the overriding priority at the front end of the lean enterprise.

## A Framework for Action

These new rules of innovation imply a broader, more flexible strategy than is typically undertaken by corporate innovation efforts. The enterprise must control huge numbers of growth opportunities to generate adequate innovation flow. It must be ready to use all means available to take advantage of unexpected market shifts.

Think of the options as a matrix bounded by control and momentum. Corporations can claim varying degrees of control (the less corporate control, the greater the potential upside) and they can tap into startups at various stages of momentum to adjust market risk (the more momentum, the lower the risk). This scheme yields three strategies: incubation (high control, low momentum), acquisition (high control, high momentum), and investment (low control, high momentum).

### Incubation

Startups that are incubated internally begin with no momentum. The onus is entirely on the innovation team to create something from nothing, and the risk is high that any given incubated startup will quickly fizzle out. On the other hand, incubation gives the enterprise maximum control. The company owns the startup, so it can motivate the team by giving it complete autonomy and a large share of the upside. The enterprise's control also manifests as the ability to handpick innovation teams and fully exploit the lean startup toolkit to move startups toward product/market fit as efficiently as possible. We look at how to manage incubation in Incubate Internally (Chapter 9).

### Acquisition

By acquiring startups that were created independently, the enterprise can take advantage of any momentum the startup already has. An early-stage startup's progress toward product/market fit may be substantial, and the enterprise can hop on a bullet train if it recognizes the potential ahead of the pack. Enterprises increasingly acquire lower-momentum startups simply to gain access to their talent. Both scenarios yield high control over the startup's direction, but not without issues. The enterprise's stake is likely to be more expensive and shared not only with the founders but prior investors as well. In addition, the founders' motivation may fall off after the acquisition, taking the momentum with it. For a closer look at the acquisition strategy, see Acquire Early (Chapter 10).

### Investment

Strategic investments give the enterprise access to high-momentum startups that may not be available or appropriate for acquisition. Buying a piece of a fast-growing startup can pay off handsomely. Case in point: Viacom bid on Facebook in 2005, but Zuckerberg didn't want to sell, and Viacom ended up without any ownership whatsoever. Two years later, Microsoft invested at what was considered an outrageous valuation, spending $240 million, or 1.6 percent of Facebook's $15 billion total worth. In January 2014 that stake was worth $2.48 billion (when putting Facebook at $153 billion at the end of January 2014). We go into more detail about investments in Invest When You Can't Acquire (Chapter 11).

Finally, there are also strategies in the low-control, low-momentum quadrant. These activities tend to fall under the loose heading of startup partnerships. For instance, RR Donnelley, a 150-year-old printing business, is the primary sponsor of Work-Bench, a "postacceleration" workspace in New York City. Young companies that already have funding and products are invited to join a six-month sales boot camp ending in a "sales day" where RR Donnelley customers can listen to their pitches. Similarly, SAP offers big-data startups that use its HANA database a stew of funding, education, mentoring, and go-to-market support. Volkswagen invites media and gaming startups to join its three-month Plug and Play Acceleration Program of education, mentoring, coaching, and introductions to potential funders. Mondelez International (formerly Kraft Foods) offers a 90-day accelerator program that connects mobile startups with brands like Oreo and Chips Ahoy.

Enterprises imagine that such timid programs will enable them to exchange soft assets such as contacts and mentorship for insights, relationships, and ideas that will help them become more innovative. But they miss four crucial points: First, as startup founders ourselves, we can tell you that startups don't want to learn from corporations. We don't want your money either—we just want to eat your lunch. Second, offering participants anything less than a chance to score a massive win keeps corporations on the sidelines of innovation rather than putting them in the game. Third, even the most powerful corporations can't provide startups with access to the early adopters who are crucial to getting disruptive innovations off the ground; startups are better off finding those customers themselves. Last, these programs offer little for enterprises to evaluate their value. So their business units get to work side-by-side with cutting-edge startups—what's that actually worth? It takes both risk and return to measure success. In the end, startup partnerships are a roundabout path toward a goal that requires steadfast commitment and laser focus.

## Fringe Benefits

Incubation, acquisition, and investment offer a number of benefits beyond any payout that may or may not be forthcoming, and you would do well to take them into account. These activities can yield:

**Insight into potentially disruptive trends**. The network you develop can focus your attention on emerging trends that might otherwise go unnoticed. Regular contact with the seed-stage investment community gives you an early window on what young entrepreneurs are working on and VCs are paying attention to. When asked how he decides what to invest in, David Lee, cofounder of the venture capital firm SV Angel, once said that he talks to entrepreneurs about what they're up to, and when he hears several say they're working on similar things, he starts looking for opportunities to invest in that field.

**A close-up view of emerging business models**. A startup's function is to discover viable business models, and sometimes these models can be generalized to fields outside of the startup's purview. Take Uber, the car service that revolves around a mobile app. The company's success has sparked many companies that can be described as "the Uber of. . .": BlackJet (private airplanes), Clutter (self-storage), Homejoy (house cleaning), Postmates (package delivery), and so on. Only close associates of Uber, however, know the ins and outs of the original winning business model.

**Access to strategic partnerships**. Acquisitions and investments can forge relationships that have disproportionate strategic value, providing access to technology that would otherwise be unavailable. By purchasing a piece of Facebook, for instance, Microsoft strengthened its Bing search engine's competitive position against Google.

**Relationships with potential future hires**. Startup veterans are battle-hardened in a way your average MBA is not, and they bring valuable perspective and experience into your company. Moreover, graduates of incubators such as 500 Startups, Techstars, and Y Combinator have completed a rigorous course in the nuts and bolts of startup entrepreneurship. To the extent that your activities bring such people into your orbit, it can pay off in access to the hearts and minds of world-class entrepreneurial talent.

**Greater visibility among potential hires**. People who choose to work for a big company self-select for nonentrepreneurial roles. They don't want the risks involved, and at worst, they aim to do the minimum amount of work to get by without being fired. People who found startups, on the other hand, are a breed apart, and the people who work for them aren't your ordinary rank and file. Many of them wouldn't ordinarily think about working for an enterprise—but they're exactly the kind of people a corporation needs to attract if it wants to innovate from within. By associating your company with disruptive innovations, whether incubated, acquired, or funded, you gain credibility as a forward-thinking workplace that embraces creativity and risk-taking.

**Association of your brand with innovation**. Many enterprise brands are considered stodgy and out-of-touch. Association with a red-hot startup through investment or acquisition can confer a halo effect in the form of headlines in tech news outlets and bragging rights on the enterprise's website. (Some large companies wait for the press to latch onto an innovator du jour and promptly buy in at whatever price. It's a hack, but it gets the job done.) Consider SAP. In July 2012, the German supplier of enterprise resource management software joined an $81 million Series D funding round for Box, an aggressive Silicon Valley developer of systems for online file storage, synchronization, sharing, and collaboration led by a charismatic CEO. That investment, along with other efforts, has helped reposition SAP as a company that understands the cloud and its implications for enterprise software.

To successfully build innovation flow through incubation, acquisition, and investment, you need an organization designed for the purpose. In the next chapter, we look at how to build an innovation colony made up of small teams that identify unexpected market trends, respond rapidly, and develop an abundance of innovations from initial inspiration to product/market fit.

**Innovation Strategy in Action**
*Case Study: Techstars, Brad Feld, Cofounder*

Techstars is a pioneering, mentor-driven startup accelerator. Since its initial 13-week program in 2007, Techstars has helped launch more than 100 companies, 90 percent of which have received follow-on funding. Today, it runs a dozen sessions a year in six U.S. cities and recently expanded into Europe. At the same time, Techstars has branched out into corporate innovation, helping Microsoft, Nike, Kaplan, Sprint, and RG/A extend their existing businesses and build new ones. Cofounder Brad Feld started his first company in 1987 while a student at MIT and went on to become an early investor in Fitbit, Harmonix, MakerBot, and Zynga. In between advising Techstars and making venture investments via Foundry Group, he has written or cowritten six startup-related books. He spoke with us about corporate innovation strategy.

### How Did You Come to Found an Accelerator, and How Did It Become a Franchise?

Every month or so, I meet with whoever wants to meet with me for 15 minutes a shot. In 2006, David Cohen, who was a local entrepreneur in Boulder arranged a meeting and described the notion of Techstars. We had no idea if it was a good idea but, together with David Brown and Jared Polis, we gave it a shot. It far exceeded our wildest expectations, qualitatively as well as quantitatively—the joy and satisfaction of working with these entrepreneurs, the fun, the intensity of the experience. By the third year, we had received about 50 requests from people in other cities who wanted to start an accelerator, too. Bill Warner in Boston dragged us to start Techstars Boston. Then we got pulled into Seattle and New York, then Chicago, San Antonio, Austin, and London. Around 2011, we did the first Powered By Techstars corporate program,

*(Continued)*

*(Continued)*

helping Fortune 1,000 companies build entrepreneurial eco-systems around their brands, products, and technologies.

### How Does the Powered by Techstars Program Work?

Many companies build a platform that allows other compa-nies to extend their products. Microsoft did an extraordinarily good job of this in the 1980s, and Facebook has done much the same thing. That ecosystem dynamic is hard for many companies to manage. And, by the way, many of the people in those companies have never worked in a startup, so they don't understand the pressures and dynamics of a startup. We come in and say, "Here's a way to help startups build stuff around your technology and infrastructure." We're an interface to those very early startup companies as they figure out how to work within a corporation's environment.

### Why Don't Established Companies Innovate as Effectively as Startups?

Established companies are good at extending existing successful product categories that they own. Clayton Christensen wrote about the innovator's dilemma, where companies defend their turf rather than disrupting it. Almost by definition, they're try-ing to get the most ROI out of products they've created rather than disrupting their industry with something totally new. You see this over and over again, and not only in the technology industry. Part of the challenge is the way organizations are set up. Part is incentives. Part is cultural norms within a com-pany: the ability to use lean startup methods, try stuff, get it out there, get feedback from customers, an iterate aggressively. That's not the way large companies work. It's not the way a planning cycle works, it's not the way to get budget dollars, it's not the way you deal with colleagues who don't want you to encroach on their area. Also, many large companies view this kind of activity as a hobby rather than as a core function of their business. These are enormous structural and cultural barriers to disruptive innovation.

***The Marketplace Appears to Be Increasingly Chaotic. Billion-Dollar Companies Rise Overnight, and Entire Classes of Businesses Disappear Nearly as Quickly. How Can Innovation Teams Cope?***

Keep in mind that the vast majority of significant enterprises still take a long time and a lot of resources to build. In the tech industry, large, incumbent companies acquire smaller, fast-growing companies to build out their teams as well as new product lines. Some buy early, when they need technology teams and don't care about the product, revenue, or customer base. But others, like Oracle, buy mature companies that have tens or hundreds of millions of dollars in revenue and significant product lines. That model can work across innovation in general.

***New Tools and Technologies Have Empowered Small Teams to Achieve Results That Once Required Corporate Departments. Do Small Teams Now Have an Advantage over Large Teams?***

I've always believed that small teams have an advantage. Organizing in small groups that use an agile model is much more powerful than working in large groups, whether it's 10 or 100,000 people. You don't have to break up the sales department into lots of different organizations, but the number of people who need to be involved in a specific decision or working on something totally new should be small.

***What Team Size Do You Recommend?***

There's no magic number, but it's important to organize according to a network model rather than a hierarchy model,

*(Continued)*

(*Continued*)

especially around new product development and launch. My whole world is a network. Techstars has 50 full-time employees, 400 companies, 1,000 entrepreneurs, 1,000 angels or VCs, 1,000 mentors—that's a big network. If you were to manage it as a hierarchy, it would be a disaster: PowerPoint decks attached to e-mails with 37 people on a chain. But if you manage it as a network, where people self-organize, where good stuff moves forward and bad stuff gets killed quickly, where you have clear ways to make decisions and mediate conflict, that's incredibly powerful.

### Is It Important to Move Fast? How Can Enterprises Do That?

It's important to move both fast and deliberately. Every startup that I've been involved with gets frustrated at some point because suddenly they're moving slower than they were at the beginning. They're not really moving slower; it feels like there's too much process because there wasn't any before. The key is not to move so quickly that there isn't any process, but to be aggressive about eliminating blockers, having lightweight ways to keep things moving, and working through the decision-making process quickly.

### Many Innovations in Recent Years Have Resulted in Winner-Take-All Markets: Google, Facebook, Instagram, Airbnb. Is There Room for a Number Two in Emerging Markets?

I don't buy that assertion. Facebook? There's also Twitter. Instagram? There's also Snapchat. However, I do believe that the vast majority of the rewards in any particular category go to the top two players. And frequently markets resegment, so number four may become number one in a differently segmented market.

### In Your Experience, How Many Swings at the Innovation Ball Does It Take to Hit a Home Run?

It varies dramatically. You have people who knock it out of the park on their first swing and others who are still swinging 100 times later. Lots of companies step up and get lots of stuff done, and others do something amazing and then struggle to do it again.

### How Are the Financing Requirements for Innovation Changing?

The amount of dollars that it takes to innovate has come down dramatically. A couple of things have driven this change. One is the falling cost of technology infrastructure required to design, develop, and build new products. Also the fact that you can abstract your compute infrastructure to a cloud host provider. The shift from waterfall to agile has also had a huge impact on costs. Methods like lean startup make it possible to measure the impact of go-to-market activities while you're in the innovation process. And there has been an incredible democratization around innovation. There are so many sources of information. Fifty years ago, it was people in white lab coats, with big R&D budgets, in big companies. Today, it's anybody, anywhere.

### What Advice Would You Give to Corporate Innovation Teams Looking to Develop Disruptive Products?

People believe they have resources that don't exist, or they think they're going to get access to resources and then don't. At the other end of the spectrum, they dive into projects without having any idea what success means. They follow a path and think they're successful, but they're not successful in the context of the business. So my advice is: Always make sure you understand what resources you have available and what the measures of success are.

# Chapter 3

# Corporate Structure

L arge companies often try to innovate within the existing corporate structure. It rarely works. The limitations on what can be
accomplished cascade from the executive imagination down to
the rank and file, affecting every aspect of product development and
marketing. We frequently work with innovation teams that aren't allowed
to talk with customers, can't allocate funds without approval from the
comptroller, or can't risk failure without endangering their jobs. We've
heard leaders at American Express say, "We can't do this because it would
put us head-to-head against Intuit." We've heard their counterparts at
Intuit say, "We can't do that because it's not what Intuit is good at."

The constraints of resource dependence, legacy competencies, and
brand identity are deadly to creativity and risk-taking. An enterprise
that seeks to be innovative must find a way to escape them. Otherwise,
it will never match the kinds of innovations that pour out of the idea
factories of Silicon Valley, New York, Boulder, Seattle, and Boston.

The ability to innovate must be built into the fabric of an organization. Innovation teams shouldn't have to think about how to navigate

the corporation to get ideas approved or resources allocated. If they have to do that, they've lost the war before a shot has been fired.

The goal of producing disruptive innovations demands a new organizational structure. Existing products, customers, markets, and competitors are irrelevant to the work at hand. Innovation teams must be untethered from the corporate identity and allowed to operate outside the corporate structure. They need a structure that not only allows but incentivizes them to look beyond the current landscape and envision a world that doesn't yet exist. Only then will the enterprise be positioned to thrive amid chaos.

## From Skunkworks Onward

Writing in 1997, Clayton Christensen recommended a way around these barriers to innovation: Build a *skunkworks*. This relatively old concept has evolved, but it remains the seed of most corporate innovation efforts.

### Skunkworks

Skunkworks (named after a smelly factory on the edge of the backwoods community depicted in the comic strip *Li'l Abner*) were pioneered by Lockheed Martin in the 1940s and later implemented by 3M, HP, Intel, and others. The idea is to pluck the best and the brightest throughout the organization and place them in a separate facility where they're assigned the task of fulfilling a predefined strategic priority. This is how Lockheed produced the X-56A, a small, fast airplane that undermined the market for the large, slow ones that the company usually built. Since a skunkworks' activity often threatens existing lines of business, it's generally kept under wraps to avoid upsetting the rest of the company.

This approach has proven successful in many cases—including wildly popular Amazon Web Services—but it's not conducive to disruptive innovation. First of all, skunkworks lend themselves to slow waterfall-style development, and lessons learned don't make their way back to the company as a whole, because of their secrecy. They can be an effective way to accomplish specific goals, but insufficient to ensure corporate survival amid unpredictable market shifts and rapidly mounting competition.

## Intrapreneurship

An *intrapreneurship* program is a more open-ended skunkworks. Instead of fulfilling a strategic priority, it aims to commercialize employee ideas. Rather than being kept secret, it's widely publicized to boost employee morale and promote the corporation's innovative spirit. Like skunkworks, these programs tend to operate on a waterfall model: come up with an idea, draw up a business plan, pitch it to an existing business unit, build the product, and become absorbed by that department. Thus, the standard of success is governed by existing business units, who push the results toward sustaining rather than disruptive innovation. Often, intrapreneurs are embroiled in department politics. In the end, they are incentivized most strongly to cater to established business units that may or may not care about bringing their innovations to market.

The story of Qualcomm's Venture Fest is a good example of intrapreneurship in action. Between 2006 and 2011, the Fortune 500 wireless technology developer solicited from the company at large up to 550 business plans a year aimed at generating disruptive innovations. Employees who submitted the plans with the highest breakout potential, as judged by peer and expert reviews, entered a three-month, part-time boot camp where they polished their ideas. Some 20 percent of the total entries were passed along to existing business units for implementation, representing hundreds of millions of dollars invested, according to Ricardo dos Santos, who ran the program.

Qualcomm Venture Fest generated plenty of interesting ideas, among them Zeebo, a low-cost game console spin-out that shut down in 2011, and Vuforia, a mobile augmented reality platform that is still under active development. Mostly, though, those ventures tended to snag on the existing corporate structure. Employees didn't know how to move their projects forward. Managers worried that the open-ended development timeline would interfere with their charges' productivity. The business units took little interest in projects that didn't fit their core competency. The R&D department (which now runs Venture Fest's successor program) gave nothing but funny looks at what they saw as ideas coming from distant left field.

"Our very success in creating radically new product and business ideas ran headlong into cultural and structural issues, as well as our entrenched R&D-driven innovation model," dos Santos writes in a blog post. Among the lessons learned, he notes the need to insulate disruptive projects from corporate politics, incentivize entrepreneurial employees, and implement "VC-like, staged-risk funding decision criteria."

### Innovation Labs

Lately, another variation has become increasingly common: the *innovation lab*. This department gathers a number of salaried intrapreneurs in a freewheeling office space that may look and feel like a Silicon Valley startup, complete with cool in-town office locations, whimsical decorations, toys aplenty, and free snacks. Innovation labs can take chances developing something fresh and unexpected, but they're not equipped to scale their successes. They can't seek outside funding, so they're at the mercy of the quarterly budget. Projects that look promising are as likely to fall prey to budgetary and political pressure as projects that don't. This exposure to internal pressures tends to keep away top entrepreneurial talent that's intent on creating a big market impact and profiting handsomely by it.

But, hey, at least the employees lucky enough to work at an innovation lab have fun shooting each other with nerf guns and perfecting their ping-pong skills, right?

The prototypical innovation lab is Xerox PARC (for Palo Alto Research Center). Founded in 1970, this legendary organization developed innovation after innovation, including the graphical user interface, the computer mouse, and Ethernet. But did it commercialize any of its inventions? No. Instead, independent entrepreneurs like Steve Jobs took those ideas and ran with them. Not an ideal model for an enterprise looking to stay ahead of the market!

For all their good intentions, we think the efforts of innovation labs rarely accomplish anything of long-term significance. They lack the autonomy, incentives, financial structure, and large pool of potential projects necessary to achieve the results accomplished by real startups. Enterprises need a new kind of organization that honors the forces that drive disruptive innovation and as well as those that drive market success. The Techstars Corporate Innovation program provides a glimpse of what it might look like.

## An Alternative Model: Powered by Techstars

In November 2011, Techstars partnered with Microsoft to run the first Powered by Techstars corporate accelerator. Hundreds of teams applied from around the world and within Microsoft, from which the company chose 11 of them. The teams were asked to conceive new products based on the theme of interfacing with Microsoft's Xbox Kinect gesture-sensing technology. They were given $20,000 each, mentorship provided by Techstars' network, and three months to develop a hit.

The teams retained 94 percent ownership of their startups and 100 percent ownership of the intellectual property they produced. Microsoft's share of the equity was structured through a limited partnership with Techstars. At the end of three months, the teams staged a demo event where they pitched Microsoft as well as outside investors on what they had produced. The teams were allowed to court funders other than Microsoft and Techstars, and in fact that's part of the special sauce. Without an open marketplace, their equity couldn't be valued properly.

As it happened, Microsoft acquired one of the teams immediately for $5 million. The surprising thing is that the team it bought came from within Microsoft itself. Rather than feeling swindled, Microsoft executives realized something profound: The existing corporate structure could not have revealed that team's tremendous value. It took the incubation process to do that.

Since then, Techstars has undertaken three additional corporate programs with Microsoft, plus programs for Nike, Sprint, R/GA, and Kaplan. The strengths of this approach are fourfold: It gives the teams autonomy to operate outside the corporate structure, it incentivizes them with the lion's share of the potential upside, it gives them access to financing on the free market, and it aggregates a large pool of startups to identify a small number of possible winners. In these ways, the corporate innovation model of the future looks less like skunkworks, intrapreneurship programs, and innovation labs and more like Techstars.

## Enter the Innovation Colony

During the European colonial period that lasted from the 1500s through the 1900s, established countries in search of economic advantage founded colonies on distant shores. These settlements were part of the mother country, yet they weren't entirely bound by its laws and customs. The citizens who moved there and the immigrants who joined them accepted the risks of the frontier in exchange for freedom, property ownership, and the opportunity to amass wealth and attain station unavailable to them at home. Many died or returned destitute to their homelands, but those who didn't return founded new nations.

We love how the colony metaphor works for lean enterprises. We propose a similar arrangement for enterprises in search of disruptive innovation. An innovation colony is an outpost where entrepreneurially minded employees and talented marketers, engineers, and designers from outside the enterprise can build new products and services, bring them to market and, share in the fruits of their success. Like a national colony, it receives resources from the enterprise in exchange for financial returns. It functions as a bridge between the entrepreneurial wilderness and the established company, offering startup founders a dynamic environment for developing new businesses while giving the enterprise access to fresh ideas and insights on emerging technologies and trends. Yet it has a distinct identity, a frontier spirit that aspires to independence and greatness. The risks to colonists are far higher than those faced by ordinary employees, but then again, the potential rewards are far greater. The innovation colony is a seed not of nations but of future businesses that will mature and become independent, to become powerful entities in their own right.

■ ■ ■

In less fanciful and more lean startup-specific terms, an innovation colony is a dedicated department of small teams focused on conceiving new products, validating the market for them, and shepherding them to product/market fit with increasing reliability and decreasing cost. It has implicit support at the highest executive levels and is recognized throughout the company as an integral part of its product development operations—in fact, it represents a significant opportunity for entrepreneurially minded employees to break out of the traditional employee/employer relationship. The aim is to test large numbers of ideas for market viability rapidly and cheaply, so the colony can be first to market with ideas that have demonstrated potential.

## A New Organization to Cope with New Rules

A colony is part design studio, part startup incubator, part corporate development department, and part investment fund. Most enterprises already have departments that fulfill some or all these functions. However, these specialized offices aren't organized to cope with the new rules that govern innovation today. First, they're an extension of business as usual, pursuing projects as dictated by top management, meaning they're not equipped to react to unexpected shifts in the market. Second, they're organized like any other department in the enterprise, not as small, agile teams that can move fast and gain first-mover advantage. Third, they're managed as separate functions, each with its own agenda. They're not coordinated in a unified effort to generate innovation flow.

The colony doesn't replace these departments but augments them with a different sort of organization. Managing incubation, acquisition, and investment as a coordinated portfolio makes it possible to apply the lean startup method throughout, consistently yielding market-ready businesses. Moreover, in a conventional company, these activities tend to be geared toward sustaining innovation, where growth is modest and disruption is a constant threat. Obviously, sustaining innovation is important and it needs to be ongoing, but the colony is laser-focused on aligning high-risk ideas with validated markets. Equally important, it's wholly separate from the day-to-day workings of the corporation and doesn't take orders from on high. It requires the full cooperation of other departments—access to data, expertise, materials, intellectual property—without compromising its independence. That's the surest path to competitive advantage and exponential returns.

The innovation colony has a predetermined quantity of capital that it uses over a fixed time period to maximize opportunities through incubation, investment, and acquisition. Incubation gives it maximum control over and ownership of high-growth opportunities. Acquisitions enable it to capture opportunities that arise elsewhere as well as seasoned entrepreneurial talent. Through investment, it can tap into startups that would otherwise be out of reach.

The cumulative effect of these activities is to create a network of skills, resources, talents, and ideas that multiplies the colony's value with each new node. The colony starts by building a portfolio of successful products, acquisitions, and investments, and these attract increasing numbers of entrepreneurs. It intensifies its gravitational pull by accumulating experience and data that makes its activities more effective. The more products incubated, the more investments, and the more acquisitions, the more valuable the organization becomes. Over time, it comes to exert a monopoly on early-stage value creation within the parameters of its innovation thesis. Organizations such as Y Combinator, Techstars, and Betaworks have accomplished precisely this, and it has generated great returns for them. It can do the same for your enterprise.

This network fills a funnel of market-ready products and services. At the wide end of the funnel, the colony scans the investment environment for promising trends, combs the startup community for acquisition targets, cultivates promising talent, generates hypotheses about unmet needs in the market and how to fulfill them, and conducts experiments to validate or invalidate those hypotheses. At the narrow end, it delivers market-tested businesses, each with a validated prototype and business model. These businesses can be spun out as independent companies, sold to the enterprise as new business units, sold to existing business units, or sold to other enterprises.

### Autonomy

The need for complete autonomy from the parent company is paramount. The colony should be housed in a separate facility, possibly some distance away. Acquired companies should be allowed to stay in their original offices rather than forced to move into the colony or corporate headquarters.

Achieving autonomy is trickier than it sounds. It means not only having permission but the capacity to act independently, and that can be as much psychological as physical and organizational. The boss may insist that employees are free to do what they want, but they'll read between the lines for limitations, and the boundaries they perceive will tend to reflect the company's historical strengths and weaknesses. So it's important to demonstrate the colony's independence in every way possible and avoid sending mixed messages.

To wit: The colony must have its own brand—an issue likely to stick in management's craw. The corporate and colony brands must be mutually protected from one another. The enterprise needs to be insulated from brand risk brought on by poor products or execution, while the colony needs to avoid association with the parent brand, which may be perceived as old-fashioned, conservative, and unexciting. In reality, the legacy brand, no matter how strong it is, has little value to fast-growing new ventures. Think of all the energetic brands that have appeared out of nowhere to attain a high profile in the past few years alone: Airbnb, Android, Beats Electronics, Spotify, Nest, Tesla, Uber—the list is long indeed.

Equally important, the colony should be its own legal entity, as should all the startups it develops. This way, they won't compete for budget against other lines of business within the enterprise, and they'll be free to reallocate ownership as needed.

In its emphasis on autonomy, an innovation colony is similar to a skunkworks, but it's a very different kind of entity. First and foremost, it doesn't take direction from the executive suite. It's not charged with executing a strategic imperative; it discovers and develops opportunities freely. Second, it doesn't profess to recruit the smartest employees in the enterprise, so it doesn't send a morale-damaging message to the rest of the staff that they're something less than they ought to be. Third, it's not secretive. Keeping secrets doesn't help anyone be more innovative. The colony is as open as any other division in the company; likely more so, given the market synergies generated by open platforms and open-source code.

### Personnel

An innovation colony starts with getting the right people in the room. These employees aren't common in the enterprise environment. They're extraordinarily creative, energetic, goal-driven, tenacious, and independent. They're motivated not by salaries, ego strokes, and holiday parties but by taking on risk and reaping the rewards. They have a drive to change the world.

Finding these people is no small task. It doesn't make sense to throw people who aren't entrepreneurially minded into an innovation colony and expect them to come up with new products. They'll see it as a "violation of their social contract," as one of our angry employees once told us. To regular risk-averse employees, being a colonist isn't about jumping in the pool to see how they like the water, rather it's a dangerous sea journey across the ocean in a rat infested ship. A colony's recruiters must be ready to screen candidates rigorously in search of an entrepreneurial A Team.

The colony's leadership is a small executive team comprising a few managing directors who combine the attitudes of entrepreneur and venture capitalist. These executives are analogous to partners at a VC firm. They report to the CEO and board on the portfolio of products and services in development. They manage innovation teams that are essentially startups, organized as cross-functional groups that have explicit authority to cross boundaries that separate traditional functional silos.

The managing directors must have close contact with the startup world and ample startup experience. Ideally, they should have contrasting skill sets drawn from business, technology, and design. Some VC firms maintain executives and entrepreneurs in residence; these can make a good pool to draw from.

Keeping this management layer stable is a huge challenge for enterprises. Hired hands who are compensated by a salary often have neither the commitment to stay in the post through difficult times nor the motivation to improve performance. The managing directors, however, must have an extraordinary degree of both commitment and motivation. If the innovation team's leaders are going to think like VCs, they need to be as committed as VCs, who personally invest hard-earned dollars in the startups they champion. The enterprise must devise a compensation strategy that compels innovation directors to put skin in the game and commit for the long term (see Compensation (Chapter 4)).

Beneath the managing directors, the innovation teams consist of three to five people likewise combining business, technical, and design backgrounds. Small teams can react *quickly* to market shifts and, as we've seen, they can accomplish as much or more than much larger teams of the past. They're cross-functional groups that avoid the silos typical of large companies. Everyone on a team is involved in all functions, especially at the beginning: businesspeople vetting designs, designers tweaking business models, technical staff driving key performance metrics. Again, the benefit is speed. The delay of waiting for approval or information from a separate department can transform a promising idea into a hollow prospect.

Innovation teams should be made up of employees who have agreed to take on personal financial risk in the interest of reaping financial rewards, and who understand the special nature of their assignment. Actually, the most creative and independent employees will learn about and gravitate to the colony naturally. One of our great-grandfathers left Spain in 1900 at the tender age of 12 years old, by himself and with just the clothes on his back. He sold his future inheritance to his brothers for a handful of coins, and jumped on a steamer headed for Havana to earn his fortune. You think he was recruited to do that?

The mere existence of an innovation colony in your enterprise gives would-be startup founders who are considering leaving to launch their own business an attractive alternative—and the company not only avoids losing capable, ambitious employees but increases profits by retaining them. (By the way, if they leave anyway, the colony should consider investing in their startup.)

You may also hire people from outside the company who possess the appropriate orientation, skills, and experience. Startup veterans wouldn't ordinarily consider working for a big company. However, the innovation colony concept may make them think twice. You're offering an innovative environment equivalent to that of a startup with a greater variety of ideas to work on, resources, and security. Strategic investments can bring the colony to the attention of like-minded people in the startup community, and you can acquire companies to bring in people with appropriate temperament, talent, and experience.

The colony's acceptance criteria should be transparent. Anyone in the enterprise should be welcome to apply, and policies should be clearly laid out for pitching ideas, terminating startups, and transferring out of and back into other business units. Those who don't qualify should know exactly what they need to do improve their chance of being accepted down the line. That way, the colony becomes a motivating force within the company rather than an elite department that breeds resentment.

Even with highly motivated employees, most startups will fail. The colony itself must tolerate failure because it's the only path to learning and thus reducing market uncertainty. However, lack of success is likely to take a toll on some team members, especially employees who are new to the colonist lifestyle. Consequently, employees' participation should be subject to renewal on a quarterly basis, and they should be allowed to return to their earlier positions, or something roughly comparable, if they find that the colony doesn't suit them. A social safety-net of sorts, their free ticket back to the old world. Tolerance for risk can wax and wane with changing circumstances. Family needs change over time. A colony team member whose startup has stalled or become stuck in neutral might wish to return to a more predictable, albeit less profitable, position.

This is actually what we think is one of the key unique strengths of a lean enterprise: an abundance of slots to fill in many different functional areas. The company should go out of its way to find a place for would-be innovators who change their mind and want to come back home.

### Funding

The ultimate function of the innovation colony is to generate high returns on investment (ROI), and for that it needs capital. However, given the extreme risk surrounding any given bet, the fund should be limited in size and time to contain potential losses. The capital should be spent before the time period is up. At that point, the colony will have reached the end of its life, and the principals will either retire or start another colony.

Allocating a predetermined amount of capital is essential to creating the sense of urgency that drives startups. A finite runway gives every action the weight of do-or-die. It makes sense to start with a small outlay to prove the concept, say $5 million over two years. Beyond that, a sensible allocation is between $20 million (the size of a typical early-stage venture fund) and $100 million over 5 to 10 years, assuming no more than $5 million will be devoted to any given startup. This range is sufficient to incubate several products or services, invest in a number of early-stage companies, and/or buy a few outright. (See Innovation Flow (Chapter 12).)

There's a benefit to keeping to the low end of the range: Having less cash to work with encourages you to move earlier and accept greater risk. The biggest expense would be acquiring a startup that has achieved product/market fit, but generally you'll be looking at targets that haven't yet reached that milestone.

The numbers should work out similarly to those of a venture fund. VCs generally take a management fee of 2 percent annually plus 20 percent of carried interest. In a blog post about the financial structure of Union Square Ventures, Fred Wilson roughs out the economics of a typical $100 million venture fund over 10 years (not actual Union Square Ventures figures):

Total Management Fees: $20 million
Total Invested Dollars: $80 million
Total Proceeds on Investments: $322 million
Total Gain on Investments: $242 million
GROSS Multiple: 4x ($322 million/$80 million)
GROSS IRR: 39.2%
Multiple Incl Mgmt Fees: 3.2x
Gain Incl Mgmt Fees: $222 million
IRR Incl Mgmt Fees: 32.9%
Carried Interest Fees: $44 million (20% of $222 million)
NET Multiple: 2.56x
NET IRR: 28.6%

Management fees account for $20 million ($2 million annually), leaving $80 million for investments that grow to $322 million—roughly four times return on invested capital. In addition to management fees, the firm is compensated by a carried interest fee. The carried interest is calculated as 20 percent of the total gain ($222 million). In total, after 10 years, the partners will make $44 million in carried interest plus $20 million in management fees, assuming the portfolio grows an average of 40 percent per year. So, assuming three partners, each makes an average of $2.1 million per year, most of it earned in the second five years.

You'll want to increase the amount of capital in play as you rack up successes and gain confidence in your innovation capacity. The more funds you put to work, potentially, the larger the management fee, the higher the carried interest, and the more capital you'll have to plow back into the operation. And there's nothing preventing you from raising funds from outside investors. You'll be building relationships with other investors if you're investing in startups, and there's no reason not to call on them if you find yourself with greater funding needs or to reduce your risk.

## Measuring Success

For many enterprise product development teams, success is measured by whether a product ships. An innovation colony has a different set of criteria. Its success depends on the degree to which it can move the needle from high uncertainty in the direction of certainty.

Let's take a look at some important metrics for tracking the innovation colony's progress.

**Number of Ideas Considered** Given the early-stage investment power law, the colony needs to draw from the largest pool of worthy ideas it can gather. The qualifications for a worthy idea are subjective. The best ideas are often laughable, so you can't base your judgment on gut instinct. However, with experience and input from experienced entrepreneurs and investors, you can gradually sharpen your intuition of which ideas are your best bets. Obviously, the more ideas you have to choose from, the better.

> The number of ideas you appraise can easily become a *vanity metric*. Accelerator programs advertise the number of applications they receive and often boost the tally by making applications easy to fill out. Don't be so eager to consider more ideas that you let your standards slip.

**Number of Experiments Performed** The faster you can run experiments, the faster you'll learn what potential customers want and how to turn their unfilled needs into sustainable businesses. Intuit runs 8,000 experiments every tax season, each one testing a hypothesis about what customers want, how they behave, and how much they're willing to pay. The result is validated learning and consequently a rational basis for allocating resources to develop one feature rather than another.

It's easy to measure improvement on this metric. You can count the number of experiments performed yesterday, make changes in your structure or process, count the number today, and compare the two. The higher the number, the more precisely you're defining your market, its needs, and its profitability. It's not a perfect measure of innovative capacity, but the experiment count is a useful indicator and an easy way to start evaluating your colony's success.

**Cost per Prototype** The prototype phase (or an intensive concierge) is an important milestone: It's the point at which you can establish baseline metrics. The cost to get an idea to this stage should be less than $50,000, assuming it takes between one and three months. This timeline allows each team to complete roughly six prototypes (or concierges that lead to baseline metrics) per year.

**Cost to Reach Product/Market Fit** This is an imperfect metric because it leaves open the possibility of developing me-too products, which are likely to cost far less than creating something genuinely fresh. Still, like the aggregate tally of experiments, it's a helpful indicator of the colony's increasing capacity to discover unmet needs and conceive offerings that genuinely meet them. The aim is to reduce this number over time.

**Return on Investment** In the end, there's no better metric than return on invested capital. If the colony chooses its startups and runs its experiments astutely, it will discover unmet needs, create products and services to match, and forge reliable conduits to paying customers. With further experimentation, it will hone these offerings into must-haves. And at that point of product/market fit, its products will take off in a blaze of glory that rains down profits like the brilliant sparks of an Independence Day fireworks display. (Well, maybe that particular flourish doesn't quite jibe with the idea of colonies, but you get the picture.) Ultimately, ROI is the true measure of enterprise innovation.

## Corporate Innovation Structure in Action
### Case Study: Qualcomm Venture Fest, Ricardo dos Santos, Former Senior Director of Business Development

Qualcomm has revolutionized mobile communications through ever smaller, cheaper, more efficient processors for mobile devices. But Qualcomm executives also recognize the need to foster disruptive innovation. As senior director of business development at Qualcomm through much of the 2000s, Ricardo dos Santos turned the company's suggestion box into an engine for developing business models outside the company's core competency. Between 2006 and 2011, he created a full-bore intrapreneurship program, including a three-month boot camp, seed investment, and a handoff to existing business units. His pioneering effort anticipated the vogue for corporate intrapreneurship programs and innovation labs and blazed a trail toward effective enterprise innovation.

### How Did You Get Involved with Qualcomm Venture Fest?

I was at Qualcomm from 2003 to 2012. In 2006, the CEO said, "Other people have ideas here. How do we create a system to hear from just about anybody?" I thought, this is an opportunity to do open innovation from within.

### How Did the Program Work?

It started as a crowdsourced website. Employees would send ideas over the fence and the executives would decide which ones they liked. But then we needed a way to move them forward. So I decided to take an entrepreneurial angle. For version 2.0, I realized that I needed both an idea and a champion, an entrepreneur type of person who would be willing to fight for their idea. When I was at MIT, I'd observed business plan competitions where they got business students working with engineering students to put together a pitch. That was my starting point, and the idea jelled over time. We received ideas from all over the company and selected the ones we thought were most interesting. The people who submitted those ideas were invited to form a small team and attend a boot camp where they were trained, coached, and mentored, so they'd have a better shot of getting their ideas heard. Finally, we put on a pitch week for the executives. At one point, we hoped, a business unit would commit the bucks to let the teams move forward with more support. I figured we could propose radically different kinds of things, even technical ideas that started as university research. We could license patents, buy startups, and we wouldn't be dependent on whatever R&D project we had underway. Let R&D take its course; here's a slew of other possibilities.

### What Role Did Lean Startup Techniques Play?

I wanted to take these amateurs and turn them into professionals. I needed a way to prepare them, so I started looking for techniques. I found the lean startup method. At the end of the day, what we were doing was similar to what startups do, trying to get investors to give them money. You don't know if you've got something until you start iterating. So I told them to pretend they were startups and taught them the basic principles. They still had day jobs, but they formed small teams and got an education in how to discover opportunities, do quick validation, and build prototypes. So the people who raised their hands saying, "I'll work on an idea on a part-time basis at Qualcomm," became the recipients of the lean startup teaching. We brought in Ideo, Steve Blank, Brant Cooper, and others to show them how to do it.

### How Did the Executives React?

They were highly impressed. They never expected to hear well put together presentations and demos and actual feedback from the market.

*(Continued)*

*(Continued)*

### How About the Business Units? Did They Pick Up the Best Ideas?

Being a business guy, I was most interested in pushing the envelope not only on technology but also business models. Be careful what you ask for! The company wasn't ready. Here comes a barrage of proposals every year, some of them asking the business units to bend over backward, at a time when they were still very successful at what they had been doing. Then the antibodies come out. Wait a minute! What are these ideas? You think R&D is chopped liver? You know, political issues. It's hard to switch to business models on a dime, and it's hard to accept ideas that didn't come from your own department. I was getting too much attention for my rank, and that created some jealousy.

### Did You Change Your Approach?

I was pruning and perfecting as I went along. I started making sure the ideas were more strategically aligned, started involving other people who eventually would have to get behind the ideas. Some things trickled through and were adopted by the company.

### Tell Us About the Biggest Successes

There was Zeebo, a low-cost game console intended for sale in developing countries. It was spun off as a joint venture with another company. The employee who proposed it was able to join and he became CEO eventually. Unfortunately, it eventually closed. It did produce and sell some product, but they couldn't make it as disruptive as it needed to be. Maybe it was an execution issue, maybe it was a flawed concept. But they tried. They put a lot of money behind it, and they learned a lot about the gaming market and making cell phone platforms into other types of appliances. But my favorite example is Blur, which became Vuforia, Qualcomm's mobile-based augmented reality platform. Qualcomm has put a lot of effort into it, and now it has a huge arsenal of computer-vision algorithms that are optimized for cellular platforms where power consumption is an issue. Now it's looking for further ways to monetize and grow the business.

Beyond those products, the CEO learned about new markets he wouldn't have encountered any other way. These projects, even if they lived for only a few months, were interesting enough. It was like, instead of paying a consulting firm for a research report, his employees gave him a research report. The CEO was like, "I didn't know cars were communicating with one another via the DSRC protocol. I have to pay more attention to what's happening in the car p2p space."

The other benefit of Venture Fest was that it stirred the pot. It put R&D on the alert: You'd better step up your innovation efforts, because otherwise we're going to lean toward these amateurs. Lo and behold, over the years, the R&D guys started coming up with some cooler, newer things.

### Why Did Qualcomm Close the Program in 2011?

At the end of the day, the CEO said, "let's give the program to R&D, let them own it and see if things get smoother." That erased the political issue. Now they've rebranded as ImpaQt. They do a couple of rounds a year and they emphasize high-level challenges that the head of R&D proposes. The R&D department follows through more readily because it owns the program instead of this independent, alien, corporate thing that I started. The danger is that they can't think outside the box or entertain business model ideas. But it's still open to anyone in the company, there's still a prep period, the executives still get to see presentations. So Qualcomm hasn't given up on asking employees for ideas. They ask employees to step forward, and they understand that it needs to be more than a suggestion in a paragraph, that they need a system where employees get to work on the early stage of the idea before it's presented for funding. Those premises remain.

*(Continued)*

*(Continued)*

### How Do You Evaluate the Program's Financial Success?

We did Venture Fest for five years, and we wrote a report every year to the executives, asking them to continue to sponsor us. By my reckoning, we put hundreds of millions into projects with easily over $1 billion in value created for the company. But it's difficult. I had a budget to farm ideas, develop pitches, and do a little follow-up work with the prize money. After that, somebody else owned the ideas and put in their money, so it was hard for me to track. Vuforia took twists and turns, and other people added to it, so it was dangerous for me to claim credit. I needed to use these things as marketing for the next year's program, but I had to learn not to say, "That's me! I came up with that!"

### What Lessons Did the Experience Leave You With?

Ideation by itself is worthless. Ideation plus acceleration is not worthless, because at least people learn a process and something of value about new opportunities. To give the best ideas a good chance of being launched, though, there needs to be an infrastructure for incubation. This can be done in a dedicated incubator, in which case you can expect not-invented-here issues when you make a handoff, or within existing business units, in which case it needs a different set of management skills and tolerance for these types of projects. The execution stage seems straightforward, but that can be complicated unless it's part of the company's strategy to diversify into new things.

So the lesson is that companies need to think systemically and holistically about how they're going to innovate. Looking at only one component such as ideation or encouraging entrepreneurship from employees might be a good start, and probably will produce some interesting proposals, but you have to be ready to follow through.

# Chapter 4

# Compensation

Entrepreneurs differ from the corporate rank and file in their creativity and independence, but they differ in another, more fundamental way: They're driven by radically different aims. Most employees are motivated by a desire for security, praise, and an opportunity to work on projects that interest them. On the other hand, entrepreneurs are motivated by autonomy and achievement.

Harvard researchers have identified two kinds of entrepreneurs. Some are driven primarily by a desire for *autonomy*, a need to be in charge with no one to lean on or blame when things go wrong. These people tend to start small businesses such as retail stores and restaurants. The other kind is propelled by a need for great *achievement*, to found new industries or build huge companies. They raise larger amounts of capital, build more ambitious businesses, and ultimately make a big positive impact on the world around them when they succeed. (They also leave bigger craters when they fail.)

Nonetheless, this second type of entrepreneur is the kind you want to attract and nurture. A rich mythology surrounds such people, but much of it is based on reality. They forego a salary, take up residence in parents' garages, take investments from friends and relatives, run up woeful debts, pitch and pitch and pitch again, refusing to take no for an answer. This is the sort of person who will go through the enormous difficulty of creating new products and bringing them to market.

## The Power of the Upside

Achievement-oriented entrepreneurs are the kind of people you need on your innovation teams. However, they almost never want to work for established companies. It isn't because corporate work is a bigger challenge than living in a dank basement and subsisting on ramen. It's because corporate work doesn't allow them to take big risks in return for unimaginably large rewards. To them, a regular job with a top-drawer salary or house-sized signing bonus is a waste of time—not because the paycheck isn't fat enough, but because the risk/reward profile doesn't align with their worldview. They're looking to risk everything for an exponential return. Figuratively speaking, they'll risk a 99 percent chance of ending up broke for a 1 percent shot at ruling the world.

> Biz Stone left behind $2 million in stock options when he left Google. Instead, he opted for 2 percent of a new venture salvaged from a failed podcasting network called Odeo. That startup was Twitter, and as of September 2013, Mail Online estimates Stone's net worth to be between $200 million to $2 billion as a result. That's what he passed up $2 million to gain.

The conventional system of compensation is broken when it comes to entrepreneurs like Biz Stone (see sidebar.) Even six-figure salaries and stock options don't make sense when a small team of highly talented and motivated people can create a company worth billions of dollars on a one-year runway. They have no incentive to give their brilliant idea to the corporation that pays their salary. They can make far more money on their own.

This is a long way of saying that if you want achievement-oriented entrepreneurs to innovate on behalf of your company, you need to give them a generous share of the upside. People who have good ideas and are willing to shed blood, sweat, and tears to make them a reality won't do it any other way. Wait! Where are you going? Don't worry, it makes sense for the enterprise as well. Management can't possibly distinguish an innovation team that's worth less than its salaries from one that's destined to be worth hundreds of millions. The only compensation model that makes sense is to pay them in a way that scales with the value they create.

At enterprises that are privately owned and that haven't set up a separate innovation colony, equity may not be available. Cases like this call for creativity. George Kliavkoff, who co-heads the entertainment division at Hearst, a private company, has instituted profit-sharing programs in lieu of equity. In the context of an early-stage company, though, such a compensation scheme might be counterproductive. You don't want the innovation team to optimize for profit before their product has reached product/market fit.

The motivating power of the upside permeates the innovation colony. Everyone involved needs to participate to some degree, from the managing directors to the innovation teams, from acqui-hires to support personnel. Let's take a look at highly motivating compensation formulas for each type of employee.

## Managing Directors

The innovation studio's managing directors are tantamount to venture capitalists (VCs), and their compensation should be structured in much the same way. They should be motivated not by a salary but by the potential upside of the startups they manage. Presumably they have a background in entrepreneurship, so they'll be accustomed to this sort of arrangement.

A typical VC's income has two components: a percentage of carried interest (a share of net return) and a management fee comprising a percentage of assets under management. The usual formula is

20 percent of carried interest and an annual 2 percent management fee. (See Invest When You Can't Acquire (Chapter 11) for a detailed breakdown of venture capital economics.)

The management fee is somewhat like a salary, insofar as recipients can count on it every year regardless of whether their fund grows. For that reason, some observers consider it abusive, and some firms go out of their way to donate management fees to charity or spend them on services for their startups. In an enterprise incubation colony, where the corporation is putting up all or nearly all of the capital, asset management is a far simpler matter than in a VC firm, which pools investments from a number of partners and limited partners. Two percent seems high in this circumstance, so a 1 percent annual management fee makes more sense. On a $20 million investment, the management fee would be $200,000 divided by, say, three managing directors, for an annual guarantee of $67,000. That will rise as they prove their success and the investment pool increases.

And the managing directors will earn 20 percent of carried interest at the end of the fund's life, say, five years down the line. By then, a number of startups should have gained significant momentum.

### Innovation Teams

Just as the innovation colony's managing directors are like VCs, its innovation teams are like startup founders, and their remuneration can follow a corresponding pattern. Founders typically take 50 percent of an appropriate salary plus a 20 percent equity stake in common stock. (Employees who come aboard after the founders often take 90 percent of their usual salary in return for the option to buy stock at a preferential price.)

Innovation team members likewise should receive a 50 percent salary plus ownership in their startups (see Incubate Internally (Chapter 9)) with the proviso that their combined equity adds up to no less than 51 percent. This arrangement gives them a modicum of security while preserving their autonomy and giving them a strong incentive to keep swinging for the fence until they hit a home run. You're giving them a shot at changing the world and getting rich in the process, and they should be willing to risk a comfortable lifestyle in return for the opportunity. At the same time, your offer must exceed their opportunity cost, giving them a better deal within the enterprise than they'd be likely to get from investors if they were to leave. The colony should let team members trade salary for equity to the limit of their risk tolerance. The pressure to perform is part of the magic that makes innovation happen.

Team members who don't fully identify with their role as entrepreneurs may be tempted to quit when the going gets tough. Such departures are costly to the enterprise, which stands to lose not only expertise but esprit de corps and momentum. To discourage departures, team members' equity stakes should vest over time. In the startup world, the typical founder's 20 percent allocation vests 5 percent per year over four years. This arrangement usually includes a one-year cliff; that is, team members who leave the company within one year forfeit their entire stake. This avoids the possibility that someone will walk away after a few months with a significant portion of the company. The equity vests 5 percent on the first day of the second year, after which it accrues linearly on a daily schedule.

### Acquisitions

Acquisitions in which you intend to maintain the company and/or its products (as opposed to acqui-hires) raise challenging issues for compensation. We cover the structure of such deals in Acquire Early (Chapter 10). As we emphasize, a critical concern is to give the founders, especially the founding CEO, ample incentive to stay on and work for the enterprise. For some entrepreneurs, an acquisition is not a triumph but a letdown, and their overriding concern is to appear successful. Compensation packages must take that into account.

Founders of acquired companies can be paid in a combination of cash and stock in the enterprise and/or the colony. Take care to structure the deal in such a way that founders aren't encouraged to retire. Lockups and earnouts, the famed "golden handcuffs," can be helpful tools for keeping critical founders involved in your colony for lengthy periods of time.

### Acqui-Hires

In acquisitions that are carried out for talent, as opposed to products, the startup itself doesn't survive the change in ownership, and its staff becomes part of the acquiring company. These people will become members of innovation teams, and they should be compensated the same way, with 50 percent of a conventional salary plus a share of equity. The portion of the acquisition price that isn't claimed by investors is divided by the team, subject to a lockup period. Depending on the terms of the acquisition, they may also receive an annual retention bonus.

As for nonfounder employees, a startup is a tight-knit team, and it's important to avoid breaking it up. A sensible approach is to increase nonfounders' take-home pay by a nominal percentage and give them options to buy equity.

### Additional Personnel

Early in the incubation colony's history, there may be no need for personnel beyond the managing directors and innovation teams. As the operation grows, though, additional employees may be worthwhile investments. In-house legal counsel can speed up acquisitions and investments; human resources management can liberate the managing directors to focus on innovation issues; and a media person can manage social media and other outbound communications. These people don't play an entrepreneurial role, so they would be hired at a full salary with stock options in the enterprise and/or colony.

---

### Compensation for Enterprise Innovation
#### Case Study: Hearst Entertainment, George Kliavkoff, Co-President

Founded in 1887, Hearst Corporation weathered the advent of movies, television, and the Internet and emerged as a prototypical multimedia conglomerate with interests in newspapers (15 daily and 36 weekly papers), magazines (*Cosmopolitan, Esquire,* and *O, The Oprah Magazine*), cable networks (A&E, ESPN, Lifetime, History), and broadcast television (29 stations).

George Kliavkoff joined Hearst in 2009. As executive VP of business at Major League Baseball and chief digital officer at NBC Universal, Kliavkoff had scored high-profile successes including Hulu, a joint venture between arch-competitors NBC Universal, News Corp, and Disney-ABC that helped pioneer commercial online television distribution. Currently, he oversees Hearst Ventures and is Co-President of Hearst's Entertainment division, comprised of TV production and cable network joint ventures (ESPN, A+E, History). He spoke with us about the incentives that drive enterprise innovation.

### What's Your Personal Approach to Innovation?

I've had an unusual approach because I've always done it within large, traditional organizations. Major League Baseball, NBC Universal, and Hearst are traditional media businesses that have needed to innovate to protect their existing businesses and grow into new ones. Most disruption comes from outside large organizations, so it's unusual to be a disruptor within large organizations.

### Do You Find That Entrepreneurs and Employees Are Motivated by Different Things?

Great entrepreneurs and great employees are similar in that they both want to win, solve real problems, and work on projects that make a difference. But they differ in their thinking about compensation. That's one of the big challenges.

### How Important Is It to Provide Special Incentives for Entrepreneurially Minded Employees?

Well, you have to, or you aren't going to attract and retain competitive folks. People who are entrepreneurial in nature want to participate in the value they create. There are so many opportunities for them to do that outside a large corporate structure that you have to be competitive. While compensation is very important to attract and retain the right people, though,

*(Continued)*

*(Continued)*

other things need to be in place before you get to the point of hiring the first person.

### What Kinds of Things Do You Mean?

I have a list of five. First, in any large organization, you need support from the very top. The CEO and board have to be behind what you're doing, or it will be doomed to failure. Second, you must have the ability and organizational support needed to build unique structures, say, to start a new company or form a joint venture with one of your biggest competitors. You have to be willing to embrace structures that don't feel right within the corporate environment. Third, it's important to have physical separation. If a corporate startup is to be successful, it can't be in the same physical location and building as the thing it's trying to disrupt. Major League Baseball is on Park Avenue; Major League Baseball Advanced Media was in a cramped space downtown in the Chelsea Market. I've gone so far as to set up companies in other cities to create that separation. Fourth, you need patient capital. You need to understand that these things aren't immediately accretive and that you have to invest to get a return. This is much easier to do in a private company. If you have shareholders who are thinking about quarterly returns, you're probably limited in the amount of forward investing you can do in new ventures. And fifth, you have to take a portfolio approach with the understanding that some projects will fail. You have to be okay with that. You can't penalize executives who work on failed initiatives. If they did a good job, you have to embrace it and move on.

### Getting Back to Compensation, How Can Enterprises Organize Their Startups to Give Employees a Piece of the Upside?

There are a few things they can do, mostly around the start-up's structure. Hulu began as a joint venture between NBC

Universal and News Corp. Then we sold a piece of the venture to private equity and created an option pool, so the employees were treated much more like traditional digital entrepreneurs than executives within large organizations. In fact, we brought in outside investors partly because we knew they would demand that the management team be properly incentivized for a digital startup, including equity. That allowed us to attract a great CEO and team. At Major League Baseball, we set up a separate company. Each of the 30 teams received a portion of the equity, and a portion was set aside to be earned by the executives who were working on that venture.

### Can You Build the Same Kinds of Structures within a Private Company Like Hearst?

At Hearst, we don't have equity plans for anyone because there's no equity to share in any of our business lines. So we have to create incentives that are as good as, if not better than, those being offered by the folks we're competing with for engineers. For instance, we've created profit-sharing plans that acted like phantom equity. Portions of the profits for every year the new venture was profitable were set aside to be shared among the employees, and all the employees had points in the plan. In some respects, that's more attractive to employees than a straight equity option plan, because it didn't require an exit to be monetized, and it wasn't a one-time occurrence. Basically it's a special bonus pool that's tied directly to the profitability of the business so that the interests of the company and the employees of the startup are aligned. It also has interesting knock-on effects. If you're the manager of that business, every time you hire a new employee and give that employee points in the bonus pool, you're diluting your own share and that of all the other employees. So you only hire someone if you think they're going to increase the pie enough to offset the dilution incurred by granting them points.

*(Continued)*

(*Continued*)

### Does Offering Different Compensation Schemes to Innovation Teams and Other Workers Create Issues around Employee Morale?

Of course. You have well-established, profitable lines of business that are throwing off cash, so you've been able to attract great talent without giving equity. Meanwhile, the people in the new venture are getting a 10 percent share. You can open that door, but it's difficult. You're going to hear from the heads of salaried business units: "Wait, I work hard for the company, I run a big P&L, why don't I get 10 percent?" You have to be ready for that.

### Many Enterprise Ceos Are Bound to Resist Spinning Off Internal Startups and Giving Equity to Employees on the Basis That These Practices Reduce the Value of the Enterprise's Own Stock. How Would You Answer Them?

Hulu was set up as a joint venture. NBC Universal and News Corp owned 50 percent each. Then we sold 10 percent to private equity. So, yes, you could say we diluted each company's equity by 10 percent. But I would argue that bringing in an outside investor established a high valuation for a company that had not yet launched. It added legitimacy that attracted and retained amazing talent to build that business. It put investors on the board who had Hulu's long-term interests in mind, as opposed to milking it for the benefit of the media equity stakeholders. So bringing in the outside investor more than made up for the dilution. When Major League Baseball created its digital wing, Major League Baseball Advanced Media, it gave 90 percent to the 30 baseball teams and retained 10 percent as a stake to be earned by the executives. If it had given 100 percent to the 30 baseball teams, the level of executive talent would have been lower and the growth of that business would have stagnated. Instead, it made the pie so much bigger that it offset the 10 percent dilution. If you give away equity without getting a benefit in exchange, sure, you're diluting yourself. But if the equity is being used to accelerate the growth of the startup and ensure that you have great talent running it then the dilution is worth taking every day of the week.

### Founders of Startups Typically Take a 50 Percent Pay Cut in Exchange for a Portion of Equity. Is This an Appropriate Model for Corporate Innovation?

It may be better to attract more risk-averse people or more risk-tolerant people depending on the nature of the business you're trying to build. If you're building a highly secure personal finance site, you probably want to attract risk-averse people, which means you'd lean toward market-based compensation on the salary side with a lower upside on the equity or profit-sharing piece. If you're building something incredibly disruptive that requires someone who is quite tolerant of risk, you probably want to attract someone who's willing to take a lower salary and willing to engage in a little bit of roulette with you on the equity upside and the profit sharing.

### People Coming from the Startup World Are Already Accustomed to That Model

Folks who are going through their first entrepreneurial experience may be looking for that kind of gamble. But the vast majority of entrepreneurial experiences don't work out. The Facebooks and Twitters of the world are the exception, not the rule. Most people who go to work for venture-backed companies never get a payout on the equity piece of their compensation. So, more often than not, folks who are doing an

*(Continued)*

(*Continued*)

entrepreneurial venture for the second or third time appreciate mitigating that risk while retaining some upside and variable compensation based on performance. They can be great
entrepreneurs even if they've been through a few unsuccessful
companies.

### Why Don't Corporations Tend to Trade Off Salary Against Equity or Profit Sharing?

It's really, really difficult. It's heavy lifting and it's painful. And it
includes embracing failure, which most executives avoid at all
cost. Part of being an entrepreneur is understanding that in a
portfolio, most things don't work out; that if you start 10 things,
6 or 7 will fail. You have to be willing to suffer the lashes of
failure to see some successes. Most executives spend their career
trying to avoid failure, not embrace it. It's a different mentality.

# Chapter 5

# Vision

## *The Innovation Thesis*

An innovation colony is designed to develop innovation opportunities into products with a ready market. But which opportunities? What criteria can a colony use to decide which opportunities to pursue and which to reject at the port of entry? The answer depends on the colony's *innovation thesis*.

Your innovation thesis is a statement of the range of ideas you're interested in supporting. It describes an area of the market that you've identified as a fulcrum of growth over a particular time period (say, the coming five years), and it summarizes the beliefs that drive your decisions to incubate a particular idea, invest in a certain company, or acquire a certain startup.

Many investors use a similar tool known as an *investment thesis*, and that's essentially the same thing. For example, Union Square Ventures' blog encapsulates its investment thesis as: "Large networks of engaged users, differentiated through user experience, and defensible through network effects." (The complete thesis statement, which is quite lengthy, can be found online.) This statement directs the firm toward businesses with a focus on user experience and network effects that might drive immense scale.

It's important to differentiate a thesis from a *theme*. A theme is a broad space such as an industry (education, health care, petrochemicals), a technology (mobile, social, or cloud), or a platform (iOS or Android). It doesn't say anything about the dynamics that affect that field. Many developers and investors choose a theme as a guide. A great example is Betaworks, developer of TweetDeck, which was acquired by Twitter. Its theme, real-time applications, has brought great success. Betaworks' connections and reputation for being ahead of the curve within its theme gives it phenomenal access to top-drawer deals, leading to investments in Airbnb, OMGPop, and Tumblr.

However, following a theme can also lead to stocking up on opportunities that fit a broad rubric without sufficient thought about the forces that are likely to drive success. It tends to promote a herd mentality as sectors and technologies become trendy. A thesis, on the other hand, broadly defines the kind of business you're interested in often without regard to industry, technology, or platform. It summarizes the market dynamics that you believe are likely to lead to success.

Your innovation thesis is a filter for opportunities, and without it, your portfolio risks drifting out of alignment with your target market. It limits the scope of the projects you work on. In this way, it's a path to learning. By directing investments toward specific types of projects, your thesis becomes a tool for evaluating whether your market understanding is accurate. Over time, it helps you develop domain expertise and pattern recognition and ultimately allows you to maximize successes and learn from failures.

The thesis is also an important communication to the outside world. When people understand what you're interested in, a community of common interest can gather around your operation and screen out those who don't share your interests. A solid thesis can also inspire people to generate ideas that you can capitalize on.

## Know the Market

A viable thesis is based on where the market is going in the future, not on what your company has proven itself to be good at in the past. So the first order of business, before you sit down to formulate it, is to become familiar with the current market.

The biggest danger lies in a thesis that's narrowly focused on the enterprise's legacy business. It's tempting for intrapreneurs to view themselves as white knights and take on the mission of extending their company's current business. This leads to a balancing act between the market, which is on its way toward breaking new ground, and the enterprise, which is desperately trying to hold onto the territory it has already captured. Much of the time, there's no profitable balance to be found. If the enterprise is in an industry that's no longer growing, the market moves on and simply leaves the company behind. Its customer base no longer sustains high growth, effectively locking it out of high returns.

On the other hand, if your thesis is too broad, you're unlikely to build up a coherent body of resources, contacts, and subject matter expertise that you can apply to future projects. The only way to build a solid foundation for innovation is to concentrate on getting to know a well-defined area over time.

To formulate a thesis that will direct you toward future high-growth opportunities, it can help to take inspiration from high-profile incubators, accelerators, and venture capital (VC) firms. Early-stage investors tend to be better tapped into emerging trends than other market participants. Accelerators like Techstars are a great resource, especially if you can sign on as a mentor. This gives you access to demo days, so you get an early look at what the next generation of entrepreneurs is thinking. Identify successful venture investors and study the theses that drive their decisions. You can usually find a VC firm's thesis on its website.

It can be difficult to evaluate a VC's success because the game isn't over until all the companies exit a particular fund. Two sources of information can help in this regard: CB Insights and MatterMark. These online services offer databases covering a vast array of private companies, their industries, and their investors. They offer real-time data such as capitalization, funding sources, growth rates, numbers of employees, and so on, as well as analytics that make it easy to compare and contrast.

This information can help you cut through the hype that fills news outlets and home in on performance metrics that matter. You can find out which venture funds have invested the most in the past year, which show the highest rates of follow-on funding, and so on. You can also identify (and avoid) zombie VCs that continue to take meetings but have no money left to invest. Armed with this data and press reports, it's not so hard to identify the firms with the best reputation and momentum. Their theses and actions can be helpful clues to trends you should be paying attention to.

Having chosen a few signal funds, consider joining them as a limited partner. Active VCs are constantly raising new funds, and if you express an interest in participating, they may well take your money as a limited partner. For instance, if your innovation colony is focused on the media market, you may join a fund that invests in media startups. Limited partners have access to annual investor meetings and unpublished research. This gives you a ringside seat that puts you much closer to the startup investment action than anyone in the press. (Invest When You Can't Acquire (Chapter 11), for more on limited partnerships.)

Published research is also helpful. For instance, Mary Meeker, a partner at Kleiner Perkins, publishes an annual report on Internet trends that delivers invaluable insights into the mobile, desktop, web, and cloud markets. Her report is a must for anyone investing in those areas.

## Formulate an Innovation Thesis

Keep in mind that your innovation thesis is a working hypothesis. It's a tool to guide the innovation studio's activities, but it's also a tool for learning, and it should evolve as you become familiar with the market and the innovation colony's capabilities. Make it a living document shared by the key stakeholders. Start with an observation about how the market is changing in the near term; say, within five years at the outset. It should resonate strongly with the managing directors' strongly held passions and beliefs.

That said, innovation theses usually revolve around the teams, the products they aim to produce, or the markets they intend to target. Starting with the team, the thesis may be something like, "Teams that have traits x, y, and z are likely to produce blockbuster products." Starting with products, it may be more like, "Products with capabilities x, y, and z will grow fastest among enterprise customers." The market-focused approach can yield a thesis such as, "Markets that are evolving in x, y, and z ways will undergo massive disruption in the next 36 months."

Have each managing director come up with three theses. Collect them and try to find commonalities among them. Then hammer out a thesis that all the directors can get behind. Finally, present it to the innovation teams and continue to work on it until everyone signs on. It's important that everyone be pulling in the same direction.

## Execute on the Thesis

At that point, it's time to put the thesis into practice. You're going to have to start executing it before you can develop a clear sense of how it relates to real-world conditions.

If you're starting from scratch, it's simplest to invest as a limited partner in a few promising venture funds. As you build your internal portfolio of internal startups, investments, and acquisitions, you'll also build your network of funders and entrepreneurs. Eventually this network will become an invaluable source of perspective about how the market is evolving, and you'll be in a position to spot emerging trends early and separate the signal from the noise. First Round Capital of New York and Philadelphia regards having a diverse network as a crucial part of its strategy. It invests its $125 million fund in a wide array of startups in the belief that breadth gives the partners access to a greater variety of entrepreneurs and markets.

Count on taking the first three to six months to hone your thesis. Let it guide a few investments, see how they go, and then revise it to better reflect what you've learned. It's critical to rely on your own experience in evaluating and sharpening your thesis. Looking at the decisions other companies have made offers little guidance to what will work for you, because you have incomplete information about what those decisions were based on. As with all things related to the lean enterprise, the watchwords are experiment and iteration.

### Case Study: Upfront Ventures, Mark Suster, General Partner

Mark Suster is one of the country's most forward-looking venture investors. He graduated UC San Diego with a degree in economics and joined Accenture, where he did systems integration for companies throughout Europe. After earning an MBA from University of Chicago, he continued with Accenture focusing on Internet and ecommerce strategy. He formed his first company in 1999, an SaaS platform for large-scale engineering and construction that was acquired by French Sword Group. He founded his second, a content management system called Koral, in Silicon Valley in 2005. He later sold it to Salesforce.com and served as that company's VP of Products. Suster joined Upfront Ventures in 2007, where he concentrates on early-stage technology companies, including investments in DataSift, Maker Studios, and Invoca. He blogs at bothsidesofthetable.com.

### What's Your Personal Approach to Innovation?

I'm an investor. It's my job to back innovators. One of the biggest mistakes investors make is thinking that they themselves have great ideas. For the most part, great investors recognize talented leaders who are innovators in their own right. As someone who built two companies and whose job is to recognize these people, though, I can offer an observation. To be able to innovate, you need a healthy willingness to challenge conventional norms. That's much harder to do than most people think. It may be beneficial for a society as a whole, but there are always people who lose. I just spent time with the leading designer of high-performance motorcycles. He expects to produce solar-charged superbikes for $15,000, and there are clearly losers: manufacturers of combustion engines, oil companies. When you go up against powerful industries like this, people fight back, and they fight back hard. It takes an Edward

Snowden, someone who understands that the only way to stand up to the system is to do something dramatic, even at great personal peril. That's what it takes to be an innovator. I see people all the time who don't want to upset the apple cart. Too many of them went to Harvard or worked for Goldman Sachs. They don't want to attack the educational institutions, industries, or general principles of the country. So they don't really innovate.

### How Important Is a Thesis or Theme in Determining What Opportunities to Pursue?

Having a strong thesis is smart. Let's take an example. It's conventional wisdom now that mobile computing is defining how applications and systems are built, and they will continue to do so. That's changing the nature of all software because it's a smaller form factor, it's personal to one individual, and it tends to know where you are. So we start with a high-level thesis that mobile computing will open up investment opportunities for people who can disrupt things that were created in the pre-mobile era. At the same time, you have two mobile ecosystems, iOS and Android, largely controlled by an oligopoly. That has to affect how you think about distribution and everything else. So, to get more granular, I believe in open platforms. I believe that Apple trying to dominate the ecosystem by forcing everything to be downloaded through its app store, where it taxes everyone's revenue by 30 percent, can't hold in the long run. I believe more open systems will emerge. So I go out looking for deals and encouraging people to approach me if they have innovation that maps to that thesis.

### What Are the Pitfalls to Avoid in Coming Up with a Thesis?

You have to consider how narrow or wide the aperture is, and be careful not to make your thesis be too prescriptive.

*(Continued)*

(*Continued*)

Too many thesis-driven investors I know think they have all the answers. They start with the answer and search for a team to match. They say, "We believe drones will have a disruptive impact on agriculture," and then search for entrepreneurs who are creating something that fits their narrative. That's too narrow; they should be scanning the landscape more broadly. For instance, I believe that television in the future will look more like Internet video than Internet video will look like television. I believe the 22-minute format is dead. The quality of content will be greatly reduced and people won't care. Story lines won't necessarily be linear; they'll be more like video games. I've published my vision of where the video industry is headed to get people's criticisms. But I'm not looking for someone who says, "Mark, we know you want videos to work more like videogames. We're building a company to your thesis." I want people to say, "I know about you through your writing, but I have this wacky idea about how video can be delivered by 3-D virtual reality glasses."

### Can You Suggest Some Guidelines for Keeping Theses from Being Too Narrow or Too Broad?

I would be perfectly positioned to answer that question if, every year, I went through a two-week process to create high-level ideas, winnow them down, and come out with 15 investment theses. But I'm not that guy.

### How Do You Go About Developing a Strong Thesis?

It requires experience. I don't think you can do it in a vacuum. I worked for many years as an entrepreneur. I observed the software market. I read Clayton Christensen's *Innovator's Dilemma* at the time that I was in a software company, trying to drive down the cost of selling and developing software and looking at how companies like Salesforce.com were bringing that into reality. You have to be open to reading other people's work, contemplating it, and trying to apply it in your own world.

### What's Your Process?

I spend time reflecting on markets and trying to learn from all the data I see. Then, when I have to codify what I know, I develop rules. That almost always happens when I have to write a blog post, prepare a presentation, or teach someone else. Then I have to say, "Okay, what do I actually think?" I'm very top-down driven in how I think, so I tend to start from a few high-level principles. One book that was very influential on me is *The Pyramid Principle* by Barbara Minto. She said that most people are data collectors. They think that eventually they'll pull all that data together and it will show trends, and from those trends they will come up with hypotheses, and then they can test their hypothesis and form conclusions. I come from the opposite school. I believe that one's experience, gut feeling, and logic should get one to a reasonable clustering of ideas. Consider a question like, "What's going to happen geopolitically because of electric cars?" Any smart, reasonably well-read person can draft a set of high-level hypotheses, and that's what I do. I take any topic that I have some knowledge of and create a high-level sketch. Then, once I top-down the pyramid, I search for evidence that proves or disproves my assumptions. Take Bitcoin: I believe a currency needs to exist to help people move money over international borders in countries that are socially illiberal. I don't know whether that's true. Then I search for whatever I need to believe in order to accept this assumption. Number one, I need to believe that people in socially illiberal countries have a strong sense that the government is hostile to their economic interests. Number two, I need to believe that they have the technological knowledge

*(Continued)*

(*Continued*)

and access to systems to buy, sell, and move Bitcoins and to understand why this could be a reasonable currency. Number three, I need to believe that their technology would have the right level of encryption that governments couldn't crack it. Then I would create the next level of assumption.

### What's Your Thesis?

My thesis is real simple. Seventy percent of my investments are entrepreneur-driven. I back someone who has a big vision for what they want to build and strong domain knowledge, who therefore is likely to have an advantage over other people, who wants to challenge the establishment and build something big, and who has the resilience not to quit when they face the inevitable challenges. Too often, people build companies to sell them. I back entrepreneurs who build companies because they want to build them. Also, I invest in deflationary economics, companies that are able to produce products that are fundamentally deflationary and that create bigger market opportunities, even though they might make lower margin and have lower overall revenues. If I look at the history of innovation on the Internet, whether it's Skype, Google, Whatsapp, eBay, YouTube, Amazon, Craigslist—they're all deflationary. They're all driving costs out of the equation and providing value for consumers at lower price points and therefore capturing very large markets that make it very hard for incumbents to challenge them. Beyond that, I invest in what I know. I see the emergence, for example, of Bitcoin, 3-D printing, and a number of other disruptive technologies, but they're not things I know well, so they don't make great investments for me.

### What Makes a Great Investor?

So much of what goes into what makes a great investor is one's incentives and what incentives you were raised on. I'll tell you a quick story about Hollywood. I went to see one of the world's top packagers of movies, TV shows, and media 15 years ago. We had a couple of lunches together and he asked me how he could get in on my deals. One day a deal came along with a very early-stage company in the media sector, so I thought he could be helpful. He said, "Okay, I think I could introduce them to huge brands in Asia. I could really help them get their early ad dollars. How much would I get paid to do that?" I said, "You'd get paid zero." He said, "I'm not going to call on all my brands and my relationships if I'm not getting paid for it." I told him, "What you get is equity in the company. By doing that, you create value that in five or eight years is going to be worth a billion dollars, and you'll own 10 percent of it rather than getting $200,000 a year for the next four years for your share of the revenue you bring in." The incentive structure of agents in Hollywood is front-end rather than back-end. I don't believe they make good venture capitalists.

### How Can Corporate CEOs Become Great Investors?

Big public companies are trained on quarterly earnings. It's about what a CEO can do the next three quarters that will raise his stock price so he makes more money on the stock. He doesn't care about 8 or 10 years. He doesn't even know if he's going to be running the company by then. Yet, venture capital is a get-rich-slowly business. You put money out for 5 or 8 years. You don't make a lot of money straight away because the average huge company that you might create takes 7 to 10 years to build. And if you do well at it, in year 11 you might start making a lot of money. Then you have to return all the capital you raised before you pay yourself. It just takes time. I wonder whether or not that's consistent with corporate structures. The best corporate investors are at Intel Capital or Comcast Ventures, where they've set up business units that are incentivized more like venture capitalists.

# Chapter 6

# Lean Enterprise Process

U ntil recently, developing new products was a haphazard affair based on a combination of past performance and gut instinct. Companies had little choice but to play the product/market lottery. The standard path for anyone seeking to bring something new to market, whether in a startup or a large company, was—and still is, in much of the economy—a long, hard slog to the public launch. You specify the offering, assemble a team, and then go into stealth mode to design, build, and manufacture it. You take the utmost care to perfect every feature; after all, if it were flawed, people might not recognize just how brilliant and useful it really was. Then, when it's polished and ready, you call a climactic press conference and release your baby to an unsuspecting public. The world is overwhelmed by your visionary genius and flawless execution. Reviewers sing your praises and customers would flock to distribution outlets to buy your creation. Profit!

Or not. Much of the time, the product sinks without a trace, and all the time, energy, and money is wasted. You may as well have gambled your capital on a roulette table in Vegas.

Eric Ries developed the Lean Startup method to avoid such dire consequences. Ries drew on ideas from Blank's process of customer development, Rolf Faste's and David Kelley's notion of design thinking, agile software development, and the Toyota Production System to create a method for developing successful businesses amid these uncertainties. The lean startup method offers a repeatable way to determine who your customers are, what they want, how to deliver it, and how to make money along the way.

The core of lean startup is experimentation, the application of scientific method to business. By following a rigorous procedure for isolating uncertainty and mitigating it, you can learn what you need to know to launch products and services that resonate with customers because they've been carefully designed to do so and tested to make sure they work.

## Roots of the Lean Startup

Before delving into the lean startup process, let's take a look at how it evolved from earlier approaches to product development. The software industry serves as a useful microcosm. In the 1970s, developers drew on techniques derived from manufacturing and construction to define the waterfall method. This method dictates a sequential process leading from specification to design to implementation to maintenance, each step of which must be completed before continuing to the next. Its methodical pace fits well with the corporate need for quarterly reports and strategic plans, and it presupposes a stable operating history that makes it possible to forecast future performance based on past accomplishments. You know who your customers are, what problems they have, and what solutions they want.

By the mid-1990s, the waterfall method's drawbacks had become apparent. It was a slow barge in the fast-moving stream of technological development. Moreover, entrepreneurs paid a high price for lack of foresight early in the process, as revisions to the initial specification based on new information or changing conditions required going back to square one and repeating each step.

The agile software development method emerged as an alternative. In this approach, designs, rather than being specified up front, evolve through a series of short, iterative cycles that allowed rapid and flexible responses to changing conditions. Agile liberated programming teams from the slow pace of corporate bureaucracy. It's well suited to creating products in a networked world where information travels in the blink of an eye. However, like the waterfall approach, it presupposes that you know your customers and their problems.

The years since roughly 2000 have brought one disruption after another: social networking, cloud computing, mobile computing, wearable computing. The pace of change has outstripped the speed of top-down management. At the same time, it has become clear that startups require a special kind of management distinct from that of established companies. In his classic book, *Four Steps to the Epiphany*, serial entrepreneur and business school professor Steve Blank observed that a startup is not a smaller version of a corporation. Where established companies know their market, startups don't know who their customers are, what they want, or how to get them to pay for it. They need a different way to bring new products to market. The lean startup method is designed to meet their needs.

### *Limitations*

As powerful as lean startup methods are, they're not without limitations. They're tailored for developing ideas from concept to product/market fit under conditions of extreme uncertainty. They're less effective to the extent that prevailing conditions are well understood. Thus, the lean startup process may not be appropriate to the following situations.

- **Legacy projects**. Projects that are *already in motion* are poor candidates for development according to lean startup principles. Decisions made without validation become an anchor that keeps the project from reaching product/market fit. The innovation colony should take on only new projects.
- **Products that have reached product/market fit**. Intensive experimentation is most effective in the early stages of product development. Once a product or service reaches product/market fit, it has a base of customers, and information sources such as customer support become the driving force behind further development.

- **Products that must match a preexisting specification**. A product designed around a specific customer's needs may leave little or no room for experimentation. If the specification is already known, there's nothing to discover, and waterfall-style development is the best approach.
- **Products aimed at regulated industries**. Lean startup methods are largely unsuitable in highly regulated industries such as medicine and finance. Tightly prescribed standards and practices will stifle an innovation colony's innovative capacity. They only way around this barrier is to produce (or latch onto) radical innovations such as Bitcoin, which skirts financial regulations due to its status as a currency independent of national governments.

### Sprints

Agile software development was a major influence on the thinking behind the lean startup method. Programmers following agile principles move their projects forward through a series of short production cycles known as *sprints*. A sprint consists of planning activities followed by execution. Afterward, the team revisits the plan and undertakes the next round of execution. A sprint typically lasts a week—long enough to get substantial work done, but not so long that team members lose their focus. This practice yields steady progress and predictable results.

Innovation teams working in a lean enterprise environment use the same framework. Like agile software development, the experimental process cycles through brief periods of learning, building, and measurement. At the end of a sprint, team members evaluate the data they've collected, adjust the product or service they're testing, and launch a new round of experiments. These cycles can be longer or shorter than a week, but that's a good place to start.

## Experimental Process: A Quick Overview

Experimentation is the heart of the lean startup method. Four things are necessary to do it effectively: a hypothesis, the riskiest assumption that underlies the hypothesis, a test method, and success criteria.

In science, an experiment tests a hypothesis to find out whether it's true or false. In the lean enterprise, the hypothesis generally states a customer problem. For the bike repair manual company, the hypothesis might be: Bicyclists have a problem getting information about how to repair their bikes while they're out riding.

Implicit in this hypothesis are several assumptions, including: Bikes break down on the road. Bikers don't know how to fix their bikes. Bikers would fix their bikes if they had the right information. Bikers carry mobile devices while they're riding. Some of these assumptions carry little uncertainty. For instance, you can be fairly sure that bicycles sometimes break down while in use.

However, other assumptions are less certain. One of them might be characterized as the *riskiest assumption* in the list: Do most bicyclists already have the information they need to repair their bikes in the event of a breakdown? If it turns out that bikers lack repair information, then you've gone a long way toward validating the hypothesis. (Some uncertainty remains, but you can mitigate it by zeroing in on the next most risky assumption.) If, on the other hand, you find that bikers have all the information they need, then you've invalidated the hypothesis as a whole. That is, you've learned definitively that, no, bikers don't have a problem getting information about how to repair their bikes when they're out riding.

To prove the riskiest assumption true or false, you need to devise an experiment. It might be a series of interviews with bicyclists. It might be collecting data on breakdowns at an observation station along a bike path. It might be an offer to preorder the mobile repair manual. Each alternative is a different way to test the riskiest assumption. It's important to choose a method that can be executed as quickly, easily, and precisely as possible. When you've completed the experiment, you analyze the results and decide whether to pivot—that is, move on to a new hypothesis—or persevere and continue to develop the idea.

Before launching the experiment, you need a clear idea of the minimum result that would validate the assumption you're testing. Would finding three out of five bicyclists who want mobile repair information be sufficient? Or would we require a larger percentage and/or a later sample? The answer is subjective, but it's not a very good idea to enter the experiment without success criteria firmly in hand. Setting success criteria helps you avoid the common traps of confirmation bias and risk aversion.

## *Confirmation Bias*

Confirmation bias is the tendency to pay more attention to evidence that confirms your assumptions than evidence that conflicts with them. People often ignore information that challenges their preconceptions.

This phenomenon is deeply rooted in psychology and has been noted by writers as far back as ancient Greece. People love their ideas, and none more than talented entrepreneurs. Salespeople are masters of confirmation bias; their work often depends on finding encouragement in signals that others would deem negative. So are entrepreneurs, the best of whom famously generate a reality distortion field that affects everything they touch. But that superpower can lead them astray when reality fails to bend to their will.

In Lean Startup Machine workshops, when we ask people how their experiments are going, it's always unsettling to hear them reply, "Everyone loves the product!" We ask whether their prospective customers signed a letter of intent, and they answer, "Oh, they would have if we had asked." Team leaders, who usually come up with the idea their team is working on, often fall into this trap. The leader says, "This is awesome," but the rest of the team looks drained and pessimistic.

A team may be struggling with negative results all day, and then a prospective customer magically tells them everything they were thinking all along. If they haven't defined success criteria ahead of time, they may well see this positive input as a vindication of their effort. But if they have, they'll recognize that one customer's enthusiasm is not sufficient to validate their assumptions.

## *Risk Aversion*

When confirmation bias is strong enough, it can lead people to avoid any situation that would call their beliefs into question. This state is called *risk aversion*, and it's deadly to performing valid experiments. In practice, it shows up as unwillingness to confront the riskiest assumption or insistence on setting up an experiment in such a way that it's bound to succeed.

At a recent workshop, one team was trying to validate a mobile app designed to mitigate long lines at coffee shops by letting customers preorder. The hypothesis was that coffee shops with long lines lost business when customers entered, saw the line, and decided to go elsewhere, and that they could use an app that made the line shorter.

The team interviewed several customers and received a lot of validation. However, the primary target of their app wasn't coffee drinkers but coffee shop managers, and they didn't interview any of those. Analytically speaking, they were approaching a two-sided market and making assumptions about both sides, but they chose to test assumptions about the less risky side first. There are a few reasons why a coffee shop manager might not want shorter lines: For instance, they might believe that long lines might attract customers rather than repelling them, and that customers would value the product more if they had to wait for it. This team avoided the riskiest assumption but never recognized the error.

In a real-world product development situation, that mistake would have led to a substantial amount of wasted resources. The solution is simple: Test your assumptions in order of risk and set clear success criteria so you know when you've validated them.

### *Documentation*

It's helpful to document your progress in testing ideas from conception to completion. At Lean Startup Machine, we've adopted three simple forms that keep team members on the same page and simplify backtracking and problem solving if anything goes awry.

1. **Idea brief.** An idea brief sets the stage for determining whether a given idea is worth pursuing. It's a page that documents your product idea, the circumstances that inspired it, your hypothesis, and a list of underlying assumptions. It serves as a point of departure for initial discussions intended to sharpen the idea, hypothesis, and assumptions. Once experimentation is underway, it serves as a reference to keep the team on track until you decide to pivot and open a new idea brief.

2. **Experiment log.** Most experiments have limitations and flaws, and a detailed record can make it easier to address shortcomings after the fact. The experiment log is a spreadsheet with spaces for noting riskiest assumption and experimental methods as well as dates, times, participants, and results. If you're tracking interviews, for instance, you may devote a row to each question and put the

various answers in separate columns, plus a final column for analysis and conclusions.

3. **Learnings report**. At the end of an experiment, take time to analyze and record the most important lessons learned: key insights, discoveries, surprises, and the like. This is the place to note customer problems you haven't previously identified—observations that can lead to the next hypothesis. It's important to collect them after the experiment has concluded. If you collect them ahead of time, you'll be recording hunches rather than validated learning.

## Experimental Process: Step-by-Step

With this summary of the experimental process in mind, let's take a closer look at each step.

### Form a Hypothesis

The hypothesis states your idea for a product or service by formulating it in a way that can be tested. One problem innovators face is that their ideas are usually amorphous and multifaceted. This makes them hard to test. One aspect of the idea might be true while other parts are false. So it's necessary to constrain the idea and state it in a clear, simple, testable form.

In the lean startup, we talk about two different kinds of hypotheses, the *problem hypothesis* and the *solution hypothesis*. A problem hypothesis asserts that a problem exists, a problem that your product is intended to solve. For instance, "A particular type of customer has a particular type of problem." Logically, if you talk to any customer who fits the description you've specified, I should find that he or she has the problem you've described. A solution hypothesis proposes that a given capability (i.e., one supplied by your product) will have a specific impact: "This particular capability will produce that particular outcome." That is, if someone uses a product that has the attributes you describe, it will bring about a change in behavior and thus a business outcome. Such statements can be tested because they posit a cause-and-effect relationship between two variables.

The first of these two formulas is best because it limits your inquiry to options that have a basis in the real world rather than imagination.

It does this by focusing on customer needs. Every customer has a problem, and every problem has a solution. There's a finite number of customers, and consequently they have a finite number of problems that have a finite number of solutions. On the other hand, every solution does not have a problem, and every problem does not have a customer—which is to say that an infinite number of possible solutions exist, many of them irrelevant to the market at large. By focusing on customers and their problems, you'll keep your ideas moored to reality.

### Identify Your Riskiest Assumption

Every hypothesis rests on a bundle of beliefs. There's no sure way to identify them all, so the best approach is simply to brainstorm as freely as possible. If the hypothesis is true, what else must be true? Give yourself ample time and mental space to record every assumption that comes to mind, and have teammates do the same. Ask for help from coaches, mentors, and people who are familiar with the market you're investigating. There's no problem if the list is repetitious or if assumptions overlap. The point is to isolate as many as you can, as early as you can.

Once you've generated a list, pare it down to essentials. Eliminate those that overlap. Remember, your hypothesis depends on these statements. If one is false, the hypothesis is, too.

Now you're ready to figure out which assumption is the most uncertain. You'll need a large piece of paper and a pad of sticky notes. Draw an x/y grid on the paper. One axis represents the degree of certainty of a given assumption, from low to high. The less information you have about it, the higher it rates. The other represents how critical an assumption is to the validity of the hypothesis, from low to high. The more heavily the hypothesis rests on it, the higher it rates. Write your assumptions on sticky notes, one per note, and stick the notes on the grid where you think they belong.

The one you've placed closest to the upper right-hand corner is your riskiest assumption. When it's time to conduct experiments, you'll test this one first and then remove it from the grid. Each time you run a new experiment, you'll test the assumption that's closest to the upper right-hand corner. This process will continue until you've either tested all your assumptions, invalidated your hypothesis, or received sufficient validation to launch a product.

## *Choose a Test Method*

There are four ways to test an assumption. It's helpful to think of them as phases to be executed in order and take them one at a time during your first several projects. As you gain experience, you can choose the one that's most appropriate to your riskiest assumption at any given point. We go into each one in depth in the chapter entitled Experimental Methods (Chapter 7).

1. **Exploration**. The first phase is exploration consisting of interviews, observation, and/or reenactment. In this method, you collect information by interviewing prospective customers or observing their behavior.
2. **Pitch**. In this phase, you're asking prospective customers to demonstrate their interest by giving you contact information, a letter of intent, money, or some other token of commitment.
3. **Concierge**. The third phase consists of manually delivering the benefits of your offering to paying customers, face-to-face. This is a real-world simulation of the product or service you intend to bring to market.
4. **Prototype**. Phase four is getting paying customers to use a functional mock-up. In this phase, you're delivering a minimum viable version of your product or service, more or less as you envision it.

There are many reasons why you might skip some of these techniques or use them in a different order. Exploration is more or less mandatory for a highly innovative project that has no obvious antecedents. On the other hand, you might skip that phase if you're starting with a high degree of domain knowledge. In that case, you can start with pitching as a way to gather customers for the concierge phase. You might go straight to prototype if you've already concierged in the course of coming up with the idea (say, users of a different product have asked for a further set of capabilities and you've been giving it to them on a limited basis) or you're innovating incrementally on an existing product category (that is, if a hardtop is on the market but no convertible).

The current riskiest assumption, too, can guide your choice. For instance, exploration is called for if you're uncertain whether people care at all about the problem you're solving. If you're certain that some people care but you're not sure how many, you might go straight to pitch. The riskiest premise might be whether you can deliver a satisfying experience, in which case concierge is the most appropriate technique. A prototype can lay to rest questions about whether the business model adds up.

The key is to choose the technique that leads most directly to learning about the riskiest assumption. The more information you have, the less risk your project poses.

## Segment Customers

Part of your experimental effort should be devoted to segmenting the market, or verifying assumptions about who your most receptive customers will be. In traditional marketing, customer segments tend to be defined by demographic characteristics such as age, gender, and occupation. A more effective approach is to pinpoint a cause-and-effect relationship between a person's characteristics and his or her interest in your offering. If you're selling pop-up basketball hoops, for instance, a demographic or physical description of target customers, such as "men under 30 years old who are over six feet tall," confuses correlation with causation. Instead, try to describe people who share a common activity, goal, or problem that would make them receptive to your offering, such as "people who live in urban areas and play basketball in their spare time."

This focus is especially important when it comes to innovative products. Your best prospects are early adopters who are on the leading edge of consumer behavior regardless of their demographic characteristics. Early adopters are defined by five traits: they're aware that they have a particular problem, they don't view it as insurmountable, they've searched for a solution, they've either used existing solutions or tried to hack one for themselves, and they don't face constraints (such as geographical or financial limitations) that would keep them from using your solution. They make an excellent resource for testing innovative ideas because they'll understand better than other potential customers what your product should do and how it should work, and they'll be receptive to a rudimentary concierge or prototype as long as it solves their problems.

Ideal early adopters are what we call cookie monsters: They're hungry for a solution and their excitement is palpable when they find one. If you find any cookie monsters, be sure to collect their contact information and share your progress with them regularly. In terms of learning, one cookie monster is worth thousands of ordinary customers.

Here's a helpful tool for market segmentation:

**Customer persona**. Commonly used in marketing, a customer persona is a fictional character who represents target users of a product or service. The document consists of a sketch with an imaginary name, idealized demographic information, and descriptions of goals and pain points. It helps the innovation team agree on who the target customers are and to get inside their heads. If you're discussing a product feature or a particular experiment, the persona can help keep the conversation focused on specific customer needs. Early in the product's life, it's best to keep personas to a minimum: You want to focus on cookie monsters. In some cases, though, you might need several; for instance, if your offering is designed for all ages, like Facebook. Don't forget to revise them as you learn more about who your best customers really are.

### Set Success Criteria

One more step prior to running any experiment: Decide on the learning that will constitute a *successful outcome*. It may include a minimum percentage of customers interviewed who confirm your riskiest assumption, number of visits to a landing page, or rise in a crucial metric. Think of an experiment's success criteria as the minimum amount of validation necessary to continue working on the project.

We became aware of the importance of setting success criteria during a Lean Startup Machine workshop when participants were giving their final presentations. A team leader proudly described the results of his team's research: 40 percent of people surveyed confirmed that they had the hypothesized problem and wanted a solution. He handed the baton to a teammate, who said, "Unfortunately, 60 percent of people we talked to didn't have any problem." For the leader, 40 percent was enough to proceed. For his teammate, it was a disappointing result. When you set success criteria ahead of time, everyone can move forward in agreement that the project is worthwhile.

Choose modest goals when you're early in the experimental process—getting one customer in 20 to validate your riskiest assumption might be enough at this stage. The more progress you make, the more you'll be able to hone in on ambitious goals. It also depends on the type of business you're testing. If you're pitching a low-margin business, you may need a high percentage of potential customers to sign up. On the other hand, if you approach 30 executives at Fortune 500 companies, you may have the seed of a viable business if only one acknowledges your target problem.

An important part of setting success criteria is limiting the time spent. This makes sense if you think about success criteria in terms of opportunity cost; the more time it takes to complete an experiment, the higher the cost. Moreover, if you run an experiment forever, sooner or later you'll get the result you imagine. Gauge the speed at which you and your team can reach the number of customers you deem necessary. Choose an interval that lets you get the job done without wasting time. Every hour counts. Remember, your competition isn't other enterprises but startups that are geared for rapid execution. That's why it's so important to work in cross-functional teams rather than silos. If you need to wait for approval from the sales department before you can talk to customers, you may as well close up shop. User experience (UX) designers in a traditional enterprise can take a week or two to conduct an interview. A lean enterprise can't afford to take that time.

Success criteria can be especially difficult to determine when you're trying something unusual for which benchmarks don't exist. In lieu of precedents, you can get by with predicting what you think will happen, based on your understanding of reality. Make a safe prediction. If you don't meet it, you will have learned that your view of reality is flawed. That will teach you about your customers, and this new understanding will lead to better decisions all around.

A little back-of-the-napkin math can help. If you plan to pitch on the street for an hour, assess the value of your time. Is it possible, given the product or service you're pitching, to nail down commitments to that amount of money? That gives you a rational basis for deciding on the minimum amount of validation you require.

You're bound to set inadequate success criteria at the beginning, so it's not worth losing sleep over. The more you do it, the better you'll get. And the more experiments you conduct, the more benchmarks you'll have to draw on.

## Build a Metrics Model

As we've seen, a metrics model is a spreadsheet simulation of your business. We show you how to build one in Innovative Accounting (Chapter 8).

This step doesn't come into play in the exploration or pitch phases, but it's worthwhile before embarking on a concierge and a must before prototyping. That's because a prototype needs to be designed up front to deliver the measurements necessary to evaluate the business. If you build the model first, you'll waste a lot of time rebuilding it once you know what variables you need to track.

## Build an MVP

Although the initial concept for your product or service may sprawl across an extensive, complicated feature set, for the purposes of experimentation, it's important to define an essential set of capabilities that constitute a minimum viable product, or MVP.

An MVP is a tool for learning what you need to know at any given moment with the least possible expenditure of resources. It doesn't need to represent the entire product, just the part you're testing at any given moment. If you're interviewing potential customers, the MVP may be a verbal description or video demo that communicates the product's value. If you're observing customer behavior, it may be a user interface mock-up or a simple landing page that gives visitors a clear idea of the product's benefits but doesn't necessarily provide access to the product itself. Even in the prototype phase, an MVP can be extremely minimal—no more than the essentials required to validate the assumption you're testing.

The prospect of presenting an MVP is a stumbling block for many companies, especially established companies that have brand equity to protect. It seems wrong to offer customers a deliberately underfeatured product or service, or worse yet, to mislead them into thinking that you've built it when your MVP is nothing more than a mock-up. It helps to realize that some customers actually appreciate a well thought-out MVP—and they're exactly the kind an enterprise innovation effort needs to reach. Early adopters are more excited by first-draft products than highly refined ones. They like to try new things. They aren't put off by bugs and they're glad for the opportunity to contribute to the design of something they want to use. So gear your MVPs toward this population. Beyond that, keep in mind the goal: maximum learning at minimal cost, so you put your valuable resources into building things that people want rather than wasting them building things that people don't want. Your job is to find the shortest path between assumptions and validated learning, and that can involve a great deal of creativity.

The MVP can be whatever you need it to be for the purpose of a given experiment. It must spark customers' imaginations and prompt them to take the actions required by the current experiment while requiring you to build as little as possible. The more quickly and cheaply you can manage that, the more efficiently you can give your customers what they really want.

### Run the Experiment

You've made a plan and now it's time to execute. This is the moment of truth. The results of your experiment will shed light on the current riskiest assumption, giving you invaluable real-world information. See Experimental Methods (Chapter 7) for an in-depth discussion of the practical aspects of various experimental techniques.

Note that every member of the innovation team is involved in conducting experiments. Everyone needs to get a feel for the product, its potential customers, and the business model that brings the two together. Progress at this stage is measured not in revenue, elegant design, or lines of code, but in how much you learn.

### Pivot or Persevere

After you've run the experiment, collect the data and analyze it. (In the prototype phase, and possibly in concierge as well, this will require plugging numbers into your metrics model.) Did the experiment meet its success criteria? If so, you're likely to persevere. If not, it may be time to pivot.

To persevere is to continue developing the idea. You've met or exceeded the minimum result needed to validate the riskiest assumption. From here, you may revise either the experiment or the offering with an eye toward eliciting stronger validation and then repeat the experiment. Or you can move on to testing the next most risky assumption.

To pivot is to go back to the whiteboard and come up with a new hypothesis. In the most literal sense, a pivot is a restatement of your business model. It's not an incremental change but a high-level shift in strategy. Tweaking or replacing a couple of features in a suite of many doesn't constitute a pivot, but scrapping all current features or reorienting the business around a single core feature does.

This isn't the failure it might seem to be. Rather, it's a clear sign of learning and an important step along the path to product/market fit. Many highly successful products and services began in a very different form than the one in which they became famous. Starbucks began by retailing coffeemakers and beans. Avon was a bookseller. Twitter began as a podcasting service. Flickr was an online role-playing game, Instagram a mobile check-in service, YouTube a video dating site. So don't be afraid to pivot. It may be your ticket to ubiquity.

You can expect to pivot frequently when you're just starting out. Early learning tends to challenge preconceptions that may seem obvious but turn out not to match up to reality. The more blind faith you have in an idea, the less motivated you are to seek out information that contradicts your assumptions. So if you're in the exploration phase and you don't pivot, it may be a sign of confirmation bias or risk aversion. Take a close look at your team and consult with mentors to avoid slipping into one of these common pitfalls.

Early on, the decision to pivot or persevere is largely a question of whether the latest experiment met its success criteria. As you get deeper into experimentation and build more validation, the decision becomes more complicated. You have a finite amount of runway, and the decision to iterate or start again from scratch is scary. Are you making enough progress toward the ideal? If not, how can you do it? Can it even be done? Team members can be at loggerheads: The engineer wants to improve the technology, the designer want to improve the user experience, the business person wants to improve the bottom line.

Use the metrics model to break such logjams. The model boils down everyone's ideas into quantitative data you can use to shed light on the best way forward. It can help answer questions about how much closer you can get to the ideal, how long it will take, and how much it will cost. When the opportunity cost of persevering becomes too great, a pivot is in order.

# Javelin Board

The Javelin Board is a tool we designed at Lean Startup Machine to help organize and guide the experimental process, and it's available as a free download from URLTK. It's a canvas that prompts you to enter information, step-by-step, as you progress from concept to validation. Use sticky notes to populate the board with brief phrases as you work. You'll be generating lots of sticky notes. Keep them brief, say, seven words at most. Not all of them will end up on the board. Keep any extra notes in a cloud off to one side. They can come in handy as your ideas solidify, especially in the event of a pivot, when thoughts you discarded earlier may take on new importance.

The left-hand side of the Javelin Board is devoted to brainstorming hypotheses. The right-hand side is for managing and tracking experiments. Note that the brainstorming fields specify a time limit of 5 or 10 minutes. This constraint isn't a strict ceiling, but it's helpful to observe time limits to keep the process streamlined and to ensure that your team moves steadily toward validating or invalidating its ideas. The lower left-hand corner offers a handful of fill-in-the-blank phrases to help you get started. They cover forming problem-and-solution hypotheses, identifying assumptions, isolating the riskiest assumption, designing an experiment, and determining success criteria; refer to them when you reach an appropriate stage in the process.

First, take five minutes to have everyone on the team write a customer description on a sticky note and paste it on the board in the field labeled, "Who is your customer?" Choose one and stick it on the right-hand side of the board in column 1, adjacent to the label "Customer."

Now have everyone on the team describe a problem that customer has, from the customer's point of view, and write it on a note. Paste the problem description on the left-hand field labeled "What is the problem?" Choose one problem, again, stick it on the right-hand side of the board in column 1, adjacent to the label "Problem."

Skip the "solution" fields for now. Instead, have everyone on the team write down five assumptions that must hold true for the problem to be valid. Put those on the left-hand field labeled "List the assumptions that must be hold true for your hypothesis to be true." Discuss the degree of uncertainty surrounding each assumption and choose one as the riskiest. Paste it on the right-hand side, in column 1, adjacent to the field labeled "Riskiest Assumptions."

Then decide on an experimental phase: exploration, pitch, concierge, or prototype. The phases generally fall into this order (which is based on how much information you have), so if the team is just starting out, in most cases, you'll start with exploration. Design an interview, observation, or reenactment to test the problem hypothesis in column 1. Write the success criteria on a sticky note and paste it on the right-hand side of the board in column 1, adjacent to the "Success Criteria" label.

Now it's time to "get out of the building"—Steve Blank's exhortation to talk to potential customers in the field. Work as efficiently as possible toward your success criteria within a predetermined time limit.

Having completed your first experiment, the team analyzes the results and uses them as the basis for a decision to pivot or persevere, as noted in the right-hand field labeled "Result and Decision" in column 1. Be sure to write down the key lessons learned and paste them just below in the field labeled "Learning."

At this point, the team clears the left-hand side of the board and repeats the process in column 2 to test a new customer and problem, this time adding a solution hypothesis.

The board includes only five columns, but that's an arbitrary limit. Continue through the loop as many times as it takes to discover a concept that resonates with customers and to develop it to product/market fit. Also, keep in mind that the Javelin Board is a simplified tool for keeping experimentation on track. The experimental method encompasses innumerable complexities and subtleties that will find their way into your practice as you gain experience with the process.

## The Lean Startup Process in Action

### Case Study: Nordstrom Innovation Lab, JB Brown, Director

The Nordstrom Innovation Lab became a lean startup sensation with a 2011 YouTube video that depicted the team using lean/agile techniques to create an iPad app that helped retail customers choose eyeglass frames. Lab personnel—working for a company that was founded in 1901, employs 50,000 people, and generated $8.5 billion in revenue in 2013—conceived, designed, and coded the app right in a Nordstrom store while customers watched, critiqued, and demoed their work. Under the direction of JB Brown, the lab fulfills strategic mandates and seeds entrepreneurial culture throughout the rest of the company. Brown, a University of Iowa software engineer who drove a pickup truck to the west coast to join the dot-com boom, explains below how he runs a classic corporate innovation lab.

### How Did the Nordstrom Innovation Lab Come About?

Brown: About three years ago, our board of directors looked deeply at the topic of innovation, and the Innovation Lab was born out of that discussion. They established the governance and funding model for a multiyear plan. I had been a developer and architect on our website for four or five years, and during that time, I'd done subversive agile coaching to increase the rate of learning and remove waste in the waterfall process. I wanted to show how technology could be used in a more aggressive manner in retailing and to show the value of a lean development process. When I heard about the lab opportunity, I hooked in and got the opportunity to start it.

### Tell Me About Your Funding, Structure, and Process

Funding is modeled after a venture capitalist approach. We have a fund set aside at the beginning the year. Anyone in the

*(Continued)*

(*Continued*)

company can pitch for use of that money, but you have to have validated proof of your idea. You're not pitching a business case. You're pitching an emergent opportunity that you didn't plan at the beginning of the year. Our innovation committee, which includes our executive management team, says yes or no. They decide whether to invest seed capital to validate your idea enough to take it further. The key factor is whether a project has the potential to improve our customers' shopping experience.

### How Big Is the Lab?

It's roughly 15 people, but it fluctuates in size. People are allowed to move out of the lab temporarily to freelance internally on a project that the lab either started or takes an interest in. We have designers, developers, ethnographers, and an industrial designer.

### How Would You Describe Your Approach to Innovation?

I take my definition of innovation from Ideo and Stanford Design School. Innovation is discovery at the intersection of what's desirable, viable, and feasible. Desirable is whether customers want it, viable is whether it's good for business, and feasible is whether we can deliver it. In that way, innovation is a virtual product, not a good, not a physical thing. The thing you build as a result of your discovery is innovative, but innovation is the discovery that made it possible.

### Innovation Labs and Intrapreneurship Programs Face Hurdles in Overcoming Legacy Corporate Structures, Politics, and Culture. How Does Nordstrom Manage Those Factors?

It can be a struggle, but it's less of an issue for us because of the decisions we made at the beginning about our funding and structure. We have dedicated funding to find new opportunities that no one realized were possible or didn't exist before. The company has various channels—mobile, stores, web—but there's space in the market for us to find new opportunities.

### How Do You Organize the Experimental Process?

The lab is broken up into studios. Each studio has a body of work and people volunteer based on the challenges they're interested in. We start with a business challenge that has been given to us by the innovation committee, a problem or an area of growth to focus on. We get to know customers and their needs, including latent needs they may not be able to describe. We observe them, and based on what we learn, we form a hypothesis about how to solve their problems. Then we brainstorm solutions, pick a couple that we think are compelling, usually with the line-of-business sponsor. If it's a mobile solution, we might get the mobile VP involved to tell us how this relates to his strategy. Then we identify areas of risk and mitigate them via MVP testing and careful innovation accounting. We view risk as volatility in the outcome, not the chance of a bad return. So we tackle the most volatile areas first by learning from each MVP attempt or experiment. We reduce volatility until our outcomes are certain enough that our leadership team gets behind them. It takes a number of iterations before we have a prototype of a solution.

### What Does Volatility Mean in This Context?

Volatility in the outcome. Customers will either love it or not. The technology either exists or doesn't. Our salespeople will either want to use it or not. If we feel like either outcome is equally likely, that's a big risk, and we want to remove it immediately.

*(Continued)*

(*Continued*)

### How Do You Identify Your Riskiest Assumption?

At the beginning, we find that the greatest risk is almost always in desirability, so that's usually the place to start. The people on cross-functional squads are knowledgeable about technology, product development, and retailing, plus we have the ethnography we've done at the beginning. Put all that together and you can make an educated guess about where volatility is the highest. The team collectively comes to a point where they feel like they know which risks are biggest and which are the easiest to remove.

### What Role Does Innovation Accounting Play in Your Projects?

We use it from the beginning. Usually, we'll pick what we think is the business model and identify the key measurements of success. At the beginning, it's a simple manual process. When we get to the point where we're trying to remove risks at a bigger scale, before going widely public, we'll use free open-source, cloud-based solutions that allow us to record metrics easily. If we get into something really complex, we'll lean on the data science lab, which is seated only a couple of feet away.

### When Would You Call in the Data Science Lab?

As a multichannel retailer, we face a challenge evaluating the impact of in-store experiences on sales. We may think we did well with a new product, where the business model is a marketing funnel and conversion happens in-store. Then we'll use the data science lab to correlate uplift in sales with our corporate data.

### Do You Worry That MVPs Might Hurt the Nordstrom Brand?

We pay attention to that. Usually our experiments start out internal and private. But at some point you have to be live, real, in public, to know whether you're getting a valid market response. Instead of going from completely private to completely public, we find ways to do semi-public experiments with small groups of customers. Sometimes we leverage our stores because we have local communities. Then we can test a small group of people compared to a bigger market. That also helps with innovation accounting because you can move from community to community, and each experiment produces a fresh cohort.

### How Do You Decide Whether to Pivot or Persevere?

This is where the art of entrepreneurship comes in. People who want to be successful have a natural tendency to persevere. It's part of our culture to make sure we're serving the customer in a way that leaves them delighted. So we've had a hard time, in the past, killing things that we thought could be successful with additional investment. I don't have a hard answer other than to gather plenty of outside perspective, watch innovation accounting, and make sure you're feeding qualitative information into your decision-making process. At some point, you have to decide where to put your money. You're never going to know the perfect answer before you do it.

### The Video of Your 2011 One-Week, In-Store App Development Project Is a Classic Demonstration of Lean Startup Techniques. Can You Give Us a Broader Sense of the Scope of Your Projects?

That video has a life of its own now. It was a great event in our lives and an important thing for our internal success, but we don't do one-week projects any more. We still focus on getting answers as fast as possible, but most of the time our objectives require us to go deeper. In late November 2013, we launched an app that we started working on a year ago. It's a texting app

*(Continued)*

(*Continued*)

that protects the privacy of salespeople and customers mutually. The law requires that texting for business use is opt-in, as opposed to e-mail, which is opt-out, so it has been difficult to put it to use. Working with our privacy and legal departments, we've come up with an app that lets customers and salespeople text one another without being able to see one another's phone numbers. We've heard from customers and salespeople that they wanted to communicate by text, so we think this solves a real problem for them.

### Do You Develop Physical Products?

We've done physical design of our in-store infrastructure. A couple of stores in California have a new beauty department design that we helped develop in response to customer feedback that our cosmetics area could be challenging to shop in. That involved physical prototyping and testing of a beauty concierge desk. Our first prototype was a table made of foam-core panels. We visited sororities here on the University of Washington campus and observed customers in a retail experience that was different from what we previously offered. We made sure that we understood the interaction between the salesperson and the customer before we spent a lot of time designing the actual prototype.

### We Feel Strongly That Innovation Team Members Should Have a Portion of Ownership in Their Projects. How Do You Handle Compensation?

The lab is part of the information technology department, and it's compensated and graded for performance the same way all other technology teams are. There's an element of truth in what you're saying, but I find fulfillment of purpose to be more important. If colleagues feel like their purpose is fulfilled, like they have the drive and autonomy to achieve it, I find that they're happy about their work. Ownership can be helpful with recruiting, but when we find people who appreciate the opportunity and the challenge, they usually accept offers that support their lifestyle, no equity needed.

### What Are Your Proudest Accomplishments So Far?

My proudest accomplishment right now is that our mind-set, our way of being, has extended beyond the lab. A small team has a built-in constraint. You're always going to have more ideas to test than one little team can do, and anything that's new and different will have its naysayers, even if they're well intentioned. It's great to get through that stage and affect the bigger organization in a positive way.

### How Have You Proliferated the Lab's Mind-Set Throughout the Company?

We offer innovation lab tours where we talk about our practices and process. We have our own version of the Lean Startup Machine, a two-day innovation boot camp that's open to anyone at the company, where we come up with a challenge and form cross-functional teams. Each team has an innovation coach from the lab who knows design thinking, lean startup, innovation accounting, ethnography, and some other things. We get people out of the building so they can talk to customers, validate ideas, and bring them to the point of being able to pitch to some senior leaders in the company. Some good ideas come out of that, but the real benefit is learning about the process and becoming comfortable with thinking in a new way. A few members of the Innovation Lab started the People Lab, and they're now separately managed to do that type of work full time.

*(Continued)*

*(Continued)*

### What Are the Most Important Guidelines for Enterprises to Keep in Mind to Increase Their Innovation Capability?

The innovation effort needs to be a well-supported, well-protected venture inside the company. You're asking for cultural change, which is not easy no matter what kind of change you're trying to achieve. While it's rewarding, it's not for the faint of heart or those looking for another silver bullet of the month.

# Chapter 7

# Experimental Methods

Experimentation is the beating heart of the lean enterprise, so it makes sense to give close attention to the methods involved. The exploration, pitch, concierge, and prototype methods are as much art as science. Mastering them requires lots of practice and careful attention to technique.

But first, you need access to customers. How can you get it? The answer depends on the kind of product or service you're testing.

For a consumer product, we tell attendees to our Lean Startup Machine workshops to go talk to people browsing at a shopping mall. For an item aimed at enthusiasts of one kind or another, they'll find a place where like-minded people congregate, either online or in the flesh. For a business service, you would cold-call workers who have purchasing authority.

The truth is, most people are petrified by the prospect of inter-rupting strangers with a request for help. It can be awkward, but trust us that it gets easier with practice. Keep in mind the urgency of learning whether your idea has legs as quickly and inexpensively as possible. Your startup is on the line, and getting input from living, breathing people is the only way to validate it.

## Where to Find Customers

Take a good long look at your customer personas, the generalized profiles that describe unique customer attributes and behaviors. The next task is to find people like that and recruit them to help validate their ideas.

The simplest way to find customers is to work your personal network and those of your teammates. Let people know you could use their help in evaluating an exciting new product they might like to use. Send out messages on Facebook, Twitter, LinkedIn, MeetUp, and/or any relevant online communities. Distribute fliers at your place of worship, health club, or social club.

Another common tactic is to approach people in public places: on a sidewalk, in a park, in a mall, outside a store or restaurant. Don't interrupt people who are clearly on their way somewhere or evince a purposeful manner. Instead, look for people who are killing time in a line or waiting for friends to arrive. You can offer them a token amount of cash to help you out, but many will be happy simply for a little relief from the boredom.

Cold calling and cold e-mailing are important techniques, and the approach is more or less interchangeable. Ask recipients if they have the problem you hypothesize and whether they're interested in learning about a solution. Tell them who you are and what you're up to. Make it clear that you're not spamming them but trying to explore a problem and a potential solution, and ask for their help.

Even knocking on doors can be effective. One company we worked with makes post office equipment. Team members dropped by the local DHL office and tried to meet with an executive on the spot. They didn't get an appointment that day, but they spoke with an assistant who scheduled time with the boss the following day.

And the Internet offers a wealth of helpful tools. SalesLoft combs online social profiles to find people who fit your customer profile, and Rapportive enriches your own contact list with tweets, job titles, and other contextual information. You can use Google AdWords to drive traffic to a landing page that describes your offering and asks visitors to enter an e-mail address if they'd like to learn more. Search Twitter for people who are tweeting about topics related to your product. A team working on an app for tourists visiting Paris used this technique to find people who were looking for things to do there

At this point, you've defined your target customers and have a sense of where to find them. Now it's time to run an experiment. All four experimental phases are on the table. You can employ exploration, pitch, concierge, or prototype (see Lean Enterprise Process (Chapter 6)) in any sequence to validate your hypothesis. Let's take a look at each one in detail.

## *Phase 1: Exploration*

The primary goal of exploration is to confirm that customers have the problem you think they have. (Look for other problems as you experiment. They'll come in handy in forming future hypotheses.) There are three major styles of exploration: interviewing, observation, and reenactment. Interviewing is the most versatile, but each is suited to testing different kinds of assumptions.

**Interviewing** Interviews can be tremendously enlightening. After all, who better to give you the lowdown on customer needs and behavior than customers themselves?

They can also be misleading and confusing. Interviews go off the rails for a number of reasons. Often people will tell you what they think you want to hear. They'll offer you guesses rather than facts, fantasies rather than realities.

Fortunately, good interview techniques can keep them on track. You'll get actionable information from your interview subjects if you stick to a few simple rules. Allocate between two hours and a full day to this technique.

- Approach individuals. You don't want to incentivize groupthink, so don't approach groups. Look for people who are alone.
- Keep your own team small. It can be helpful to have an assistant to take notes, but people will be more receptive if you approach them by yourself.

- Start positive. Begin the interaction on an affirmative note by opening with a line that they're likely to answer with a "yes," for instance, "Isn't it a beautiful day?"
- Set a time constraint. Your marks will be more receptive if they don't feel trapped into a long conversation, so it helps to establish a false time constraint. Something like, "I only have a minute, but when was the last time you used social media?" or "Do you have 20 seconds to answer one question?" Don't be shy about asking more if their initial answer contains useful information.
- Ask questions about how your subjects have behaved in the past. When was the last time you shopped online? What did you buy? How satisfied were you by the service? Generally, statements about the past are more accurate than statements about the future. Ask people how many times they'll go to the gym in the coming year, and you're almost sure to get wishful thinking. Instead, ask how many times they've worked out in the past year. You're much more likely to get a realistic reply.
- Avoid asking leading questions. You want authentic answers, not the ones you expect. One way to do this is to pose questions with open-ended answers. In other words, not "Do you like Groupon?" but "How do you discover deals?" If you ask yes or no question, not only will you learn less, you'll unintentionally encourage subjects to give you the answers they think you expect. Similarly, don't ask people what they think of your idea. Asking for feedback is likely to lead to poor data. Generally, people want to be positive and optimistic. If they feel uncomfortable criticizing you, they aren't going to answer honestly.
- Stay away from hypothetical questions. Never start a question with "would": Would you use a wireless mouse with your mobile device? Would you ever download a shopping-list app? You want to know about real-world behavior: Have you ever had problem x? Tell me a story about the last time it happened. Consider starting questions with when, what, where, how, and why:

  When was the last time you experienced a dropped call?
  What were you doing at the time?
  Where were you?
  How did you solve the problem?
  Why have you stayed with your current mobile provider?

- Focus on your subject. Don't take notes while talking to people; that's a turnoff. If you need to record the interaction, use an unobtrusive recording device and be sure to let interviewees know you're doing so.
- Listen, don't talk. It can be hard to get used to listening when you want to tell people about your exciting product. However, the aim of interviewing is to hear what others say. Give interviewees space to speak. Allow silences to linger after their replies—they may yet have more to say.

**Observation** Asking people how they behave is a convenient way to understand their behavior, but watching them provides a much more accurate picture. Observation is an ideal method when you're inclined to distrust what people tell you, you want to gather spontaneous reactions, or you need to learn about complex actions that don't lend themselves to memory and verbal description. Think of this option as a way to avoid asking hypothetical questions: Just put people in a situation and see how they behave. It should take no more than a half day.

For instance, we worked with a team that wanted to learn whether people in a retail environment would use their smartphones to scan a quick response (QR) code in return for a reward. They got permission from the store manager to display a QR code on a store counter. Then they watched to see whether shoppers noticed the display and how they responded. Another team set up a sign in a shopping mall offering a URL for people who had a particular problem, and looked for people to enter the URL in their mobile browser. Both teams received real-world information about how potential customers actually behave, as opposed to how they say they behave.

**Reenactment** Some problems strike infrequently or unpredictably, making them difficult to observe. Sometimes they arise from complex circumstances that are difficult to create. In these cases, you can discover how customers behave by reenacting the situation. Reenactment can be time-consuming, but in many situations you can complete it within a half day.

For instance, you might want to learn about problems that arise when filing an insurance claim after an auto accident. Asking people on the street to describe their experiences would risk the likelihood that few interviewees have experienced an accident in recent memory. Observation wouldn't be very helpful, as you'd likely wait at an intersection for a long time before witnessing a collision.

It would be much more effective to advertise for people who have been through this experience and lead them through a reenactment. You need not crash their car. Instead, you'd lead them through an imaginary accident and its aftermath, taking time to fill out all the necessary forms and noting their reactions, difficulties, and questions.

### Phase 2: Pitch

You've validated the target problem through exploration. The next phase is to validate demand by selling your solution (even though you haven't built it yet). When you pitch, you're looking for a demonstration of intent or commitment to buy. The goal is to get customers to give you something of value, such as an email address or a letter of intent, in return for a promise of access to your product or service. You might spend as much as three days on this phase.

Following up exploration with a pitch can test the quality of your Phase 1 results. One team we worked with included a salesman who was tall, handsome, and suave. Other people on his team who interviewed prospects encountered a lack of interest, but his interviewees were always enthusiastic. They moved to the pitch phase and set up a landing page asking people to sign up for their service. It fell flat. The team concluded that their good-looking colleague's results were anomalous. There might be other reasons why the landing page didn't perform—perhaps it was badly designed or written—but, in this case, the initial exploration was clearly misleading.

In later sprints, you can use the pitch phase to discover a repeatable source of customers. Demand depends on your customer acquisition channel, and the better that channel is, the more effectively you can validate demand. Even if your idea addresses a real customer need, if you can't find a repeatable way to reach the right customers, it won't fly.

**Throwing the Pitch** The sales channels you use are up to you. You can pitch on the street, at public events, via cold calls, on a web page—anywhere that gives you access to customers. (Here's a tip: If you hold up a sign in a public place, you might be asked to leave. So print your pitch on a T-shirt and wear it. No one will be able to chase you away.)

Incidentally, Lean Startup Machine offers a landing-page tool that can automate the pitch phase for online products and services. Other tools are available for landing page design, but they don't help when it comes to finding early adopters and validating your ideas. QuickMVP is a free authoring environment for quickly building single-page websites that demonstrate purchase intent. It leads you through all the steps from domain registration to reporting results, and it includes call-to-action buttons that let customers download files and enter addresses or credit card numbers. You can find it at quickmvp.com.

Your offer will be most persuasive if you put it in language your customers understand, so you should know your audience well before you undertake a pitch. When people consider a product, the first thing they ask themselves isn't "What good does this do?" but "Is this for me?" Make sure your pitch leaves no doubt by aligning your sales script, landing pages, and other sales materials with their activities, goals, pain points, and overall orientation. Testimonials can be a powerful tool in this regard, because they use a customer's own words.

**Demonstrating Intent to Purchase** It's important to get the customer to give up something of value, be it a nominal amount of cash, time, contact information, or some form of comfort. If you were offering a product or service for free, most people would accept it because there would be no risk involved. Demonstrating a commitment, on the other hand, requires putting something on the line.

Choose a currency appropriate to your target customer. You might ask consumers at a mall to give you an e-mail address in return for the opportunity to buy your product at a discount. For business-focused products, getting an executive's time may be sufficient, but you can also ask him or her to sign a nonbinding letter of intent to buy when certain conditions are met. All the better if you can get people to give you money—that's a solid demonstration of intent to buy. (Note that the strength of a purchase commitment is relative to the person making it. A payment of $50 from a CEO represents a small commitment, whereas getting the amount from a teenager is huge. Conversely, two hours of a CEO's time is a substantial investment, while the same amount of time with a teenager is likely to mean little.)

The best currency for a given pitch may not be obvious. A participant in one of our workshops wanted to sell genetic data to pharmaceutical companies, but he wasn't sure how to collect it. He had already raised venture capital and had developed a viral social game that required participants to enter their hair color, eye color, and so on. He hit the street, asking people to play the game. To his surprise, no one was interested. So he devised a different strategy: He asked people whether they would promote scientific exploration by spitting into a cup. This time, people were happy to oblige, and he was able to collect much higher-quality genetic data at a much accelerated pace. For the purposes of his project, saliva was a much more effective currency than a few minutes of time and attention.

You may not deliver the goods regardless of the currency you receive. In that case, you'll send your customers a gracious note of apology along with a refund of any money they gave you.

### Phase 3: Concierge

After pitching, you should have customers queued up. Now it's time to deliver the benefits of your product—without building it.

The concierge method consists of delivering the solution manually via face-to-face interaction with customers, with as little product development as possible. Where exploration validates the problem and pitch validates demand, concierge generally tests customer satisfaction. What's the most convenient way for them to access the product, what features do they use most frequently, and how do they feel afterward? The concierge phase answers questions like this. This method can take time, especially if you use it to iterate on product features, so count on taking between a week and three months.

Manual Rossi used this method to build a successful smartphone app called Food on the Table. The app creates a shopping list based on the diners' food preferences, what's on sale at local grocery stores, and a library of kitchen-tested recipes. Rather than build the app right out of the gate, Rossi charged his early customers $9.99 a month to sit with him at a coffee shop working through mock-ups of the user interface, poring over grocery store sale circulars and cookbooks, and drawing up lists of items to buy. Whenever customers hit a snag, they figured out how to streamline the process and tried again. Customer by customer, Rossi learned how to deliver a satisfying, scalable service that has served more than 1 million customers as of January 2014. (Rossi is an extreme example. He automated each facet of his process only when it became impractical to execute manually. He grew the business to 200,000 customers when the app was fully functional.)

Concierging can reveal hidden issues that may be masked in the exploration phase. One developer we worked with hypothesized that small business owners who advertised job openings didn't have time to sort the resumes they received. He received more than 1,000 commitments to buy a product that would solve the problem, so he skipped directly to building a prototype. When he showed it to customers, though, they found it confusing. He concierged to figure out what the problem was. He sat down with a customer and a stack of resumes and asked, "What criteria should I use to sort candidates?" The customer didn't know! The problem wasn't that employers didn't have time to sift through resumes, it was that they didn't know what they were looking for. The time he spent developing the prototype was wasted.

**The Wizard of Oz** A variation on the concierge method known as the *Wizard of Oz* is especially well suited to apps and online services. When Dorothy first visits the Wizard in the 1939 Hollywood classic, the Wizard appears as a fire-breathing head that floats in mid-air. Later, the dog Toto pulls back a curtain to reveal a flustered old man pulling levers and turning dials to create the demonic illusion. In a Wizard of Oz concierge scenario, you're the person behind the curtain. Customers believe they're receiving an automated service, but behind the user interface, you're doing everything manually.

Sometimes you don't even need to do the work manually; you can fake it in other ways. Paul Howe, founder and CEO of NeedFeed, used a clever Wizard of Oz ploy to test his idea for a Facebook app that let members notify friends when they made a purchase. His interviews had yielded mixed signals. Prospective customers told him, "I wouldn't use it, but I'm sure someone would." So he decided to test that proposition. He hired a programmer to code a JavaScript that made his browser insert made-up messages into the real Facebook newsfeed, plucking friends' names from the currently signed-in account: "Your friend John Doe just bought an iPod." Then he invited prospective customers to sign into their accounts and noted their reactions. The results were resoundingly negative. Out of 50 people, only three liked being told what their friends were buying.

The silver lining behind this tale is that Howe had two direct competitors who didn't bother to test the idea and spent $10 million each building the app. Nine months later, they both threw in the towel—and Howe had a nine-month head start on his next idea.

### Phase 4: Prototype

Entrepreneurs who aren't aware of lean startup principles often build a prototype first. But mocking up a product doesn't make sense until you've fully tested your hypothesis through a number of concierge runs. Only when you've validated a problem, demonstrated demand for a solution, and verified that customers find your solution satisfying is it time to build a prototype. The good news is that by the time you've taken those steps, you should have a clear idea of what you need to build.

Prototyping need not take much time early on. In keeping with the idea of a minimum viable product, it should embody only the essentials that make your product or service compelling and allow it to grow into a sustainable business. That said, the implementation must be solid enough that you can gather high-quality data about how customers interact with it. If the crucial features are incomplete or buggy, they won't teach you what you need to learn. This phase can be as short as a few days or as long as a month.

The prototype phase is always preceded by building a metrics model (see Innovation Accounting (Chapter 8)). By the time you've learned enough to build a prototype, you should be in a good position to figure out the critical measures that describe how users interact with your offering, how it delivers value, and how new customers discover it. It's important to bake these measurements into the prototype so you can plug them into the model and evaluate your progress toward product/market fit.

**Prototyping Process** Start by drawing up a complete specification of the capabilities you plan to deliver and the metrics that will reflect how well the plan is working. You can expect to make revisions after your initial experiments, but the fundamental design priorities should not result from an iterative process in this phase. Take care to think things through thoroughly so you don't waste time later redesigning, rebuilding, or sorting through ambiguous results. For instance, if you're building a freemium product, you need to include the upgrade option or else you'll have no way to judge whether your business can scale. Likewise if you're building a viral product; if your viral messaging system leaves out the "sent from . . ." signature, you won't receive an accurate measure of the product's viral potential.

Maintaining a disciplined build–measure–learn loop is paramount in the prototype phase. First build, then measure, then draw conclusions and solicit user feedback that will help you increase the behavior you want to encourage (and thus the metrics you seek to increase) on a targeted basis. It's easy to get lost in the weeds if you fail to hold to this process.

One team we worked with discarded a promising idea because the team members never definitively limited the scope of what they intended to build. Their product was a social customer relations management tool, and they found a number of early adopters who were excited by the idea. However, in designing their metrics model, they didn't isolate essential features and figure out how they would generate a scalable business. Instead, they built a prototype and asked users for general, qualitative reactions. Naturally, they received conflicting information and random suggestions. So they revised the product accordingly. Upon asking for the next round of feedback, they received an equally diffuse critique. The product concept wandered as they tried to implement various user suggestions. Ultimately, they lost sight of their own vision and gave up. They missed a solid opportunity because they failed to set up a clean execution plan and stick with it.

A number of tools are helpful in making the transition from concierge to prototype. They prompt the team to think about various interactions between users and their offering and how to shape those interactions to achieve the desired results.

**Hook Canvas** A product of Nir Eyal at the Stanford Graduate School of Business, the Hook Canvas is a template for designing products and services that spur high engagement, or what is commonly called *addictive behavior*. (That's the "hook" part.) The idea is to deliver triggers (say, an e-mail reminder) that lead to actions (such as clicking on a photo) that lead to rewards (perhaps further photos of interest that may be beautiful or surprising). When this sequence is repeated, the user internalizes the triggers and the use pattern becomes habitual. The canvas serves as an aid to product design by laying out this scheme in a form that lets you fill in the blanks for the interactions you want to generate. The hook canvas fits into a growing movement of behavioral design spearheaded by Stanford's Persuasive Technology Lab.

**AS IS Journey Map** A customer journey map outlines the process your target customers go through as they experience a problem and solve it. The AS IS format, which focuses on the customer experience as it is currently, makes this quick and easy. It divides their experience into steps, identifying at each stage what customers do, think and feel, and want and need. This formulation helps you keep your focus on the customer experience as you build your product or service. Make one AS IS Journey Map for each customer persona (see Lean Enterprise Process (Chapter 6)), and be sure to base it strictly on information gleaned from exploration, not on your impressions of what customers go through.

**TO BE Scenario** Where the AS IS Journey Map considers the present, the TO BE Scenario describes the future. It describes what happens to customers who use your product from start to finish, describing how their experience changes as they use it. This is a good tool to use if your offering isn't intended to produce highly engaged (daily or weekly) use, but it's useful for addictive products as well. If you include the Hook Canvas' triggers, actions, rewards, and investments in the narrative, you can integrate the TO BE Scenario with your work in that tool.

**Six Up** This tool combines personas with the TO BE Scenario. It simply presents pictures of six people using the product in different ways and describes each one's experience. This is helpful for a product that's intended to cover multiple use cases.

Taken in order, with many iterations in between, the four phases will lead you to a thorough validation—or invalidation—of your hypothesis. You can also use them out of order, but we advise you to consider that an advanced technique. A disciplined process to experimentation will lead you to product/market fit by the shortest possible path.

---

### Case Study: Comcast Silicon Valley Innovation Center, Preston Smalley, Executive Director, Product Management

Take the world's biggest media company, with a commanding presence in cable TV, broadband Internet, telephony, and movies. Add a dot-com startup struggling to retool for a new era of Internet and mobile applications. Result: Comcast Silicon Valley Innovation Center, formed in 2011 to align the Philadelphia-based cable provider with the forces of technological disruption. Comcast, founded in 1963 and now 12,000 employees strong, acquired Plaxo, a cloud-based address book, in 2008. Preston Smalley joined two years later. After reorienting the division toward agile software development and demonstrating the power of lean startup methods, he helped found the Innovation Center. Today, he and his 250 colleagues are cranking out new products at the nexus of mobile, social, and cable networks. He took time to speak with us about lean startup experimentation.

### Tell Us About Comcast Silicon Valley Innovation Center and What You Do There

Comcast set up the Innovation Center a few years ago. The company realized that innovation around TV, home automation, and Internet connectivity would be driven by technology and software development. It acquired Plaxo, an online address book, to turn those activities into core competencies, and that became the basis of the Innovation Center's engineering,

*(Continued)*

(*Continued*)

product, and design talent. I came here to be the general manager of Plaxo, and that's where I cut my teeth on how to do
lean startup methods. It was clear to Comcast that what we
were doing made sense, so they talked me into repositioning
my team to work on more Comcast-focused products. Now I
run product management, working on mobile apps and next-
generation TV applications, sometimes in partnership with
other Silicon Valley companies.

### How Did You Learn About the Lean Startup Method?

I went through an experience at Plaxo that really brought
me to my knees. At the time I joined, Plaxo was running
flat. They'd built an online address book and tried to pivot to
being a social network, hoping to compete with Facebook
and LinkedIn until it became clear that it was a winner-take-
all situation. So we talked to customers, trying to figure out
what to do next. A lot of people said, "My address book is a
mess. It's completely out of date. I have different people on my
phone and a computer, I have duplicates, and everything is out
of sync. Please help me."

So we doubled down on our original value proposition
and set an audacious goal of building a machine-learning system that would automagically figure out the most up-to-date
info for all your contacts based on the wisdom of crowds
and a host of data sources. But what we thought would be a
six-month project turned into 18 months. When we finally
showed it to the same customers, they were like, "It's nice, but
I'm not willing to pay $10 a month for it."

The company continued to go sideways, and we had
wasted most of the team's time for a year and a half. At around
that time, I picked up Eric Ries' book, *The Lean Startup*, and it
hit me like a ton of bricks: *We never tested whether people would
pay for the product!* We could have tested our solution hypothesis

long before we worked on heavy lifting around technology. I could have had a person in India updating people's address books manually and I would have learned immediately that this isn't something people are willing to pay for. Many of us have a messy closet, but we don't stampede the closet-organizing store to get the stuff to fix it. We manage through it.

### What's Your Personal Approach to Innovation?

My background is in computer engineering; I spent seven years running design at eBay, and along the way I got a business degree. For me, innovation happens when I'm seeing overlapping trends, I see a customer problem, then I hear about interesting technology, and I see a business opportunity arise out of that.

Here's an example. Right now, people want personalization in their entertainment experience. They want Comcast to know what movies and shows they're interested in and to make recommendations. But we don't know who's watching, because no one wants to log in and out of their TV. Meanwhile, I'm seeing Bluetooth Low Energy come forward as a lightweight way of cookie-ing and tracking people. I'm thinking, if we could layer those two things onto each other, we'd have a platform that told us who was watching what, we'd be able to personalize the experience for them, and that would be worth a lot of money as a business—not only as an experience, but also as an advertising platform. Seeing those three worlds of business, tech, and the user overlap to spark an innovation.

### How Do Your Projects Move Through the Experimental Process?

We think about our projects like a VC would. We go through a seed stage where we evaluate a project. If it looks good, we

*(Continued)*

(*Continued*)

seed fund it, which means we put a couple of people on it for a month or so. If they're able to prove their hypothesis, we give them "Series A" funding to let them build what we call a minimal testable product, not quite viable, but testable enough that we can learn something from it. If that goes well, we might do a "Series B" in order to build an MVP. All the while we're looking for an exit. We don't want to be in the business of having to run all these things, so we look for another team within the company that we can hand off to. We'll give them a successful MVP that they can continue to scale.

### What Percentages of Your Experimental Efforts Are Devoted to Exploration?

Roughly 10 to 15 percent of our effort consists of user interviews and other exploration, 15 percent pitching, 15 percent concierging, and 55 percent prototyping.

### How Do You Find Prospective Customers?

It depends on who we're trying to reach. If we're bringing people in locally, we've had some luck with Craigslist. If we want to deploy something in the field, we have a trial team that was set up to try new set top boxes in the field. They can hand us existing Comcast customers who say, "I'm interested in doing studies." They work at a much larger scale—like, one-third of the Bay Area would get a new set top box—but we have used them in smaller-scale settings. We also recruit through advertising on Facebook. We did that for a product called BirthdayGram that addressed a market adjacent to Plaxo's. The idea was to have all a person's friends record little video messages, and we would stitch them together into a single video and post it on the person's Facebook wall on their birthday. We thought that our early adopters would be teenagers and college students, and we also wanted to find people who would be ready to put themselves on camera. So we did a Facebook ad campaign for girls who were in the right age bracket and liked to dance.

### What Role Do Observation and Reenactment Play in Your Experimentation Process?

We do in-home ethnographic research. We did some observation around family communication. We wanted to understand how families, especially families with teenage kids, communicate. How do they talk about their schedule? How do they get in touch with each other during the day? We followed families around and watched them interact. That led to an MVP app called Family Connect that lets families share messages and calendars with one another. They can say, "I need to be picked up," and post a picture of the location. They can push a button and enter a party line; it calls everyone in the family so they're all on a conference call together. That concept came from user observation.

### What Tips Would You Offer for Successful Customer Interactions?

Trying to get people in their natural environment where you can see what they do rather than what they say they do. I know a guy who used to work on Tide at Procter & Gamble. Whenever he asked people how they washed their clothes, they always explained how their mother taught them: "I separate the whites and colors and do each load separately." But when he watched them, he saw that they just dumped the clothes all together. If you didn't watch them wash their clothes, you wouldn't realize it, so Procter & Gamble had to make a detergent that worked well in a mixed environment like that.

*(Continued)*

*(Continued)*

It's the same problem we had at Plaxo. People say, "I love to have a clean address book," but they don't really care.

### What Form Do Your Pitches Usually Take? Do You Use Landing Pages, or What?

They start verbally. They could be sketches or screenshots that we've mocked up, like a paper prototype. Those are the primary ways until you get into concierge or Wizard of Oz prototypes.

### What Tokens of Customer Interest Have You Collected, Such as E-Mail Addresses or Credit Card Numbers?

One very helpful thing we've done is ask people to choose between keeping the product we'd given them or taking a gift card. For instance, in the early stages of the music video app project, we asked, "For $5, which would you rather have? This app that lets you tune to music videos on your TV or a $5 iTunes gift card?" It was easier than deciding whether to buy a service for $5 per month, because most teenagers don't sign up for monthly services; that's the parent's role. Either I'm going to have this service or get this gift card. It gave us a way to determine what the service was worth to a teenager.

### Under What Circumstances Would You Build a Prototype?

You build a prototype either because you're not sure how the customer will respond or you're not sure whether the technology is feasible or how useful it would be. The Bluetooth Low Energy prototype was like that. We wanted to see whether we could tell whether users were in their living room, kitchen, or bedroom, since those locations would imply different things about how they would use their TV. The prototype worked well and now we're going to try it with customers.

### *What's Your Approach to Building Prototypes?*

We do it three ways. One is to hack together a solution out of other vendors' products. For instance, we recently tested a concept for a music video application. People love watching music videos on the TV but it's hard to look for specific ones. We were trying to place that activity in a group context to see how multiple teenagers would interact together in a jukebox/afterschool scenario. So we hooked up an Apple TV with the Vevo video app running on it and brought in 10 teenagers. They had never used that technology, so for all they knew, we had built it.

Sometimes we bring in people to use technology we've developed on our own. And sometimes we might deploy a functional product to a limited number of customers, say 20 to 30. For the music video project, we built a TV remote that ran an app similar to Spotify and delivered it in the field. We tried it with 20 teenagers in the Midwest. We realized that they liked it, but they wouldn't use it enough. The data taught us that if we wanted to go that route, we needed to either go full bore into music or make the music video functionality a feature of a broader remote control setup.

### *Can You Offer Tips for a Successful Prototyping Process?*

I just had this conversation with my team yesterday. You shouldn't prototype something that's obvious or unsurprising, something you know you could do, how it would work, and how the customer would respond. You want to test the riskiest elements of your plan.

### *Do You Use Innovation Accounting in Conjunction with Concierging and Prototyping?*

I'm looking to use it more. We're keeping track of how much we've spent on a given innovation, how many man-weeks

*(Continued)*

*(Continued)*

we've spent on a given project, to understand what our outlay is and weigh it against other opportunities. We're also looking at the eventual revenue opportunities for the company.
That might not be straight revenue that improved retention or
improved acquisition of customers.

### How Do You Insulate the Enterprise Against Brand Risk from Minimum Viable Products?

We do three things. First, we launch products under a separate brand. BirthdayGram, while it was covered under a broad
set of Comcast policies, was positioned as a separate brand and
you'd have to dig to understand that it was Comcast. Second,
we launch under a brand called Comcast Labs and tell the
customer explicitly that these things are experimental technologies that we may get rid of or incorporate, and this is your
opportunity to play with them. Third, we have a variety of ways
of trialing and a/b testing with customers. We can do it in small
samples, certain regions, special contexts where we can see how it
plays out before it gets scaled to tens of millions of customers.

### How Do You Decide Which Approach to Use?

One heuristic is how much brand risk the product poses. The
greater the brand risk, the more likely we'll go with a separate
brand. Another is how likely the new product is to be folded
into a mainstream product. If it's likely to go mainstream, we're
more likely to use Comcast Labs or possibly trial it under the
proper Comcast brand. The sooner you want to roll out that
feature, the closer you are to the Comcast brand, and vice versa.

### Can You Tell Us About a Time When a Prototype Led to a Pivot?

Recently we set up a partnership with Twitter to launch a nation-
wide social TV service called SEEit. Twitter's audience likes to

discuss TV, yet Twitter is disconnected from how people watch TV. We have many ways to control a TV remotely over the Internet, but it's separate from the conversation on Twitter. So we worked with Twitter to develop an app that, when people tweet about TV, a button appears that will record the show, tune a TV that's in front of you, or let you watch on an iPad. That service evolved in a lean-startup way from a concept to an initial prototype, but we pivoted before releasing the MVP about a month ago.

### How Did You Pivot?

Initially the product was focused on cable TV. When users clicked the button, they needed to identify who their TV provider was, and then we worked with the TV provider to create an experience that was tailored to them. Time Warner would power one experience, we'd power another, DirecTV would power another, and so on. As we saw how many clicks it took to go through that process, we recognized that we needed to create a provider-agnostic experience that didn't ask those questions up front. We also realized that we needed to pull in the programmers who created the content—ABC, NBC, HBO, or whoever—and integrate their apps deeply into the experience as well. Their apps may or may not already be on the user's device, so we didn't want to create a barrier at the very beginning of the process. That required us to change our business development posture in terms of how we reached out to TV providers versus programmers.

### What Did You Learn from the Experience?

That experience taught me that you need not only great innovators but also great business development. There's an interesting synergy between my team in Silicon Valley, Comcast's business development minds on the East Coast, and great partners like Twitter. Together, we've tackled challenges that nobody else has been able to crack.

# Chapter 8

# Innovation Accounting

According to traditional accounting, business success is measured by the bottom line: Specifically, revenue that outstrips expenses, the bigger, the better. But what if you're still discovering what business you're in? You don't yet know precisely what your product will be, who will use it, what they'll use it for, or where the money will come from. You have no revenue, margin, or profit and no financial history that suggests a timeline to profitability. Your spinning wheel company may be growing steadily in value, but years may pass before it starts turning straw into gold.

Under these conditions, traditional accounting shows no difference between a startup that's failing and one that's on the verge of breakout success. You may be hatching the next Pets.com, or you may be witnessing the dawn of the next Facebook. Which is it?

Innovation accounting gives you a way to assess the difference, creating accountability and transparency in an area that was previously ambiguous. This lean startup technique allows entrepreneurs to track their progress and financial decision makers to measure the market potential of their investments.

Rather than financials, innovation accounting is based on measurements of user behavior. It reveals whether the business is growing in ways that matter for financial success in the long run: What percentage of visitors to the site return, what percentage take advantage of standout features, what percentage become paying customers? These metrics form the basis for a spreadsheet *metrics model* that lets you forecast an ideal case and compare that to actual performance over time. In this way, the model lets you make sensible projections, evaluate whether the venture is meeting them, and ultimately make decisions about whether to persevere with the original plan or pivot to a new one.

Metrics are appealing because they constitute hard evidence of whether a business is viable. But choosing the right ones to track can be tricky. There's no cookie-cutter template of behavior that drives every product. It takes as much effort to understand the metrics around a product as to develop the product itself. Serial entrepreneur Dan Martell estimates that fully 30 percent of a startup team's time should be dedicated to looking at metrics and building tools to help better understand them.

The rise and fall of turntable.fm illustrates the point. Launched in May 2011, the social DJing service became a viral sensation, gathering 360,000 monthly active users in a mere three months and accruing a valuation of $37 million. The service was addictive (as we can personally attest). But it also required a high degree of user involvement either DJing or critiquing the current DJ's selections. Users couldn't afford to devote their full attention, especially during working hours, and soon they began leaving. An astute metrics model would have measured the variables most important to the site's viral growth: What percentage of visitors become registered users? How much time, on average, do registered users spend on the site? What's their attrition rate over time? If the metrics had shown that user engagement was falling precipitously, the founders might have added features that, say, made it easier to step in and out of the experience. Instead, the user base evaporated, and the developers shut down the service and pivoted to focus on producing live online events, with an uncertain future.

The crucial measurements for any given project depend on the product design, business model, and customer psychology, and it takes care and practice to recognize and model them in a way that sheds maximum light. A few concepts can be helpful in thinking through these issues: vanity versus actionable metrics, pirate metrics (a fun name for numbers that describe a customer's progress from window shopper to loyal patron), and engines of growth.

## Vanity Metrics versus Actionable Metrics

Businesspeople often concentrate on what lean startup mastermind Eric Ries calls *vanity metrics*, numbers that sound impressive but don't reveal much about the underlying business. Vanity metrics tend to be totals: total number of dollars, total number of page views. Tech news sites are full of vanity metrics. A TechCrunch headline trumpets, *Google+ Hit 10 Million Users in Two Weeks*. Ten million users is an impressive number, but it says nothing about how long they stayed, whether they returned, how often they returned, and what they did that might be monetized. Google+ may sign up a thousand times as many people and still fail because, after registering, they never come back. Similarly, the fact that a company has raised $100 million in venture capital tells you only that the firm is good at fundraising, not that it's a good business. Its total revenue tells you that it can get customers to open their wallets but not whether its business is sustainable.

Furthermore, vanity metrics lend themselves to being gamed. Before a meeting with investors, founders might ask blogger friends to publish favorable write-ups or buy Google ads to yield a timely boost in site visits. The visitors may not sign up for their service, or getting them to sign up may cost more than they'll ever pay, but the founders have made the point: Their startup is a roaring success!

On the other hand, *actionable metrics* reflect user behaviors that are critical to growth. These numbers are actionable because they help you make decisions about how to prioritize new features, allocate resources, adjust pricing, and so on. They tend to be per-user averages: average usage per customer, average profit per customer, and so on. For instance, for a photo-sharing app, an actionable metric might be the average monthly number of snaps uploaded per user. For a car-sharing service, it might be the average monthly tally of hours per customer that cars are in use. The total number of customers can be quite small and still yield valid perspective on how the business is progressing and how to make it grow faster.

We've found that the distinction between vanity and actionable metrics is less about the metrics themselves than the context in which they're presented. If you simply claim 10,000 registered users, you're offering a vanity metric. But if you add that 3,000 users registered last month and each one referred an average of three friends, the 10,000-user claim makes a case that your product has viral potential.

## Pirate Metrics

Another way to look at metrics is in terms of measuring customers' journey down the marketing funnel. Well-known angel investor Dave McClure categorizes measurements depending on whether they relate to customer acquisition, activation, retention, referral, or revenue, or AARRR. Speak the acronym out loud and you'll know why he calls his scheme "pirate metrics." The goal is to move people through the funnel in the highest possible volume, at the lowest possible cost.

- **Acquisition** is the transformation of people into customers. Online, it happens through a visit or registration. In a retail environment, it happens through a purchase; in a service setting, through a signed contract. Important acquisition metrics relate to channels that bring potential customers including search engine optimization, public relations, advertising, contests, and so on.
- **Activation** refers to the transformation of new customers into happy customers. There's no way to verify this objectively, so how you measure it is up to you: a particular amount of time spent, a certain number of page views or clicks, a certain amount of money spent.
- **Retention** encompasses measures of customer loyalty, including return visits, subscription renewals, duration of membership, and so on. Retention metrics include e-mail open rates, RSS click-throughs, and visits or other activities over a graduated series of time frames after signup (say, 3, 7, and 30 days).
- **Referral** is simply the rate at which customers send new people to your offering and how active those referrals are. Viral products depend on this dynamic.

- **Revenue** is self-explanatory. Any measurable action that affects revenue belongs in this category, including the rate of response to upgrade offers, automatic product recommendations ("if you liked that, you'll also like this"), and the like.

The pirate metrics framework is a useful starting point for determining the numbers that need to be included in a metrics model. However, the specific measurements depend on design, user psychology, and especially the product or service's engine of growth.

### Engines of Growth

In conventional practice, to sell a product, you need a sales team; the bigger the team, the more of the product you can move. In a networked world, however, some products virtually sell themselves. Their design incorporates what Ries calls an *engine of growth* that drives sales automatically, and fine-tuning the engine can make growth lift off. A product's engine of growth offers clues to the actionable metrics that need to be included in its metrics model.

Online products, especially, tend to use one of three types of engine. The definitions are a little fuzzy and often overlap. Fundamentally, though, a product or service can be *viral*, *sticky*, or *paid*.

- **Viral**. This engine of growth is driven by referrals. Using a viral product is tantamount to sharing it. Skype fits this description. If you want to use it, the parties you want to call must have it as well. If they don't, you'll ask them to download the software, and they have a good incentive to do so in return for free phone service. Or Dropbox: To share files, you need people to share them with, and if they don't already subscribe to Dropbox, you'll send them an invitation. In modeling a business like this, focus on metrics that reflect the relationships between sharing, invitations, and new signups.
- **Sticky**. In businesses based on the sticky engine of growth, the product stimulates high engagement, and users become enmeshed in ways that make for prohibitive switching costs. Revenue depends on upselling to increase the customer's lifetime value by offering enhancements, accessories, and package deals. Legos are a great example. Customers invest in building blocks that fit only with one

another, and then they're enticed by specialized parts that extend the value and utility of the standard blocks by letting them construct thematic scenarios (animals, holidays, superheroes, Star Wars).

- **Paid**. Companies based on the paid engine of growth use revenue from customers to pay for advertising and other customer acquisition channels. A dating website is a typical example. It's not sticky because customers use it only until they find a steady date, and it's not viral because generally they don't want to tell their friends lest they make a negative impression. The most important metrics are the lifetime value per customer and acquisition cost per customer; the business can remain viable as long as the former exceeds the latter.

A particular business's engine of growth provides clues to the variables that will make an effective metrics model. In a viral product, for instance, the rate of new sign-ups (typically viewed as a vanity metric) is less important than the rate at which current users take the actions that lead to new sign-ups (which are considered actionable metrics). A model made up of measures like these conveys a clear picture of how customer interactions with a product relate to business growth. Tracking them over time gives you a rational basis for deciding whether they have potential to drive a sustainable business.

## Building a Metrics Model

A metrics model gives you insight to the measures that are most important to any given offering. It shows you how a change in one metric affects the business as a whole. This insight helps you determine which parts of the model are riskiest and thus most important to fine-tune. Whereas traditional financial metrics are too small to be meaningful when small numbers of customers are available, a metrics model can convey a clear sense of the business's potential with even a handful of users.

Note that building a model is a crucial step prior to developing a prototype minimal viable product (MVP)—especially a software prototype—and, depending on how fully you've validated your solution, it's a step that you undertake before delivering a concierge MVP (see Experimental Methods (Chapter 7)). The model provides developers with a list of customer actions that must be measured by the MVP. If you take these steps out of order, you're likely to waste substantial time and effort retrofitting the MVP to gather the data your model calls for. So be sure to have the model ready before you begin developing a prototype or concierge MVP.

To build a model, start by identifying actionable metrics that reflect the customer journey through the marketing funnel and how they function in the relevant engine of growth. Some are fundamental—things like the rate of visits, sign-ups (acquisition), usage (activation), returns (retention), invitations (referral), and payments (revenue)—but it takes careful analysis to choose a selection that reflects the way your particular solution generates value for customers and growth for the company. Answering these questions can illuminate the relevant metrics:

- How will customers find the product?
- When they find it, what percentage will try it?
- When they try it, what percentage will be happy with it?
- When they're happy with it, what percentage will upgrade or pay?
- How often will they use it?
- Will increased usage lead to paying for additional services or features?
- Can the company become profitable quickly enough to invest profits in advertising or sales?
- Is the product only usable or valuable when used with friends?
- Does the product's value improve with additional customers?

Once you've built a model, you'll populate it with fictional data; numbers that represent a case that, in your judgment, constitutes a viable business. This is known as the *ideal case*, though it's not necessarily ideal. It's a case you'd be happy to see, one that's optimistic but achievable.

Specifying the ideal case is similar to setting success criteria before running an experiment. You're making a prediction about how the model will behave in the real world. The difference between your forecast and real-world performance serves as valuable feedback to your understanding of the market. It also helps you avoid the pitfall of retrospective coherence (the psychological tendency to view events, in hindsight, as having confirmed what you knew all along).

Next, over a series of sprints, you'll collect real-world data to replace the fictional numbers. The initial real-world measures are known as the *baseline*. (These measurements are likely to come from prototype or concierge experiments. The research and pitch methods tend to generate qualitative information that doesn't lend itself to plugging into a model.) Each sprint should close the gap between the ideal and the baseline by deploying a new feature or improving an existing one. The model will help you identify user behaviors worth encouraging, and as you fortify them, the real-world metrics should approach the ideal.

> Many people seem to believe that the way to improve business performance is to improve the user experience. But if you improve the UX of a product or service that customers hate, they'll only come to hate it faster. The only rational way to improve performance is to identify actionable metrics, make experimental adjustments to the product, and see whether the numbers move in the desired direction.

At the end of each sprint, analyze the data, extract the lessons learned, and make a decision to pivot or persevere; that is, to continue developing the project or start over with a new hypothesis. Some products will reach a plateau where their performance isn't moving closer to the ideal on a weekly basis, or the baseline may be so far from the ideal that it's not worth pursuing. In these cases, a pivot probably is in order. On the other hand, if your experiments are successful, each week will bring the product's performance closer to the ideal. When the real-world numbers match or exceed the ideal case, you'll have a solid indication of product/market fit.

### Tutorial: Modeling an Online Subscription Business

Let's build a metrics model for a product sold by subscription. We've laid the foundation by conducting experiments that validate our hypothesis that a particular set of customers has a problem, and that our product solves it in a way they find satisfying.

Customers sign up to receive a daily package of five unique articles. They pay nothing for a version that includes advertising, but they can pay $15 monthly to receive an ad-free version. The enterprise has an existing business unit that generates the raw material, so we can license it and package it. If and when the business reaches the metrics profile that confirms product-market fit, the enterprise can acquire the startup and scale it up by advertising on a preexisting high-traffic website.

Experiments indicate that the price is right and that the business will acquire new customers virally when users share portions of the product designed for this purpose. We'll probably make a small amount of money per user, so we'll need a high volume of users. The question now is whether we can grow the business large enough to generate a compelling profit. The model should answer this question.

Open a spreadsheet. Rows are metrics, columns are weekly sprints. Let's fill in the cells and establish the ideal case.

The first set of metrics represents customer acquisition channels. We're driving a small amount of traffic via Google Adwords (*impressions from Adwords*), so we count on gathering 100 potential customers weekly from that source. Sharing by users will drive further traffic (*new referral traffic*). We plan to boost traffic with special promotions if necessary (*promotion traffic*), but for now they're not important.

We expect 10 percent of total traffic to convert to sign-up for an ad-supported free trial (*acquisition rate*), yielding 10 free accounts in the first week (*total accounts*).

We've defined activated customers as those who read articles on four days within the first two weeks, and we expect 40 percent of customers to activate (*activation rate*). On average, these customers will share two articles weekly through social channels that reach 10 friends (*referrals per week*). This activity yields an average of five views per article.

Based on previous concierge experiments, we've established that one-third of activated customers will pay the $15-per-month fee for ad-free articles (*percentage of new accounts that become paid*), yielding seven paying customers in the first week. The more a customer uses the product, the more likely he or she is to upgrade to the paid version.

Concierge tests also revealed that customers who read at least four articles a month like the service enough to continue almost indefinitely, so we expect 99 percent of activated customers to stick with it (*weekly retention rate*). This is a highly addictive product.

These interactions yield a tiny amount of advertising revenue (*average advertising revenue/free user*) and $9 per paid user (*average revenue/paid user*), totaling $36 in the first week. At this point, the monthly run rate is $144.

Extending the model out 10 weeks shows that it's not a viable business: The monthly run rate at week 10 is only $4,182. We might advertise for new customers, but the model shows that this would yield

|                                        | 1      | 2      | 3    | . . . | 9       | 10          |
|----------------------------------------|--------|--------|------|-------|---------|-------------|
| Impressions from media properties (weekly) | 100 | 100 | 100 |     | 100     | 100         |
| Recurring Referral Traffic             | 0      | 0      | 0    |       | 0       | 0           |
| New Referral Traffic                   | 0      | 100    | 240  |       | 2578.56 | 3475.36     |
| Promotion Traffic                      | 0      | 0      | 0    |       | 0       | 0           |
| Total Traffic                          | 100    | 200    | 240  |       | 2679    | 3575        |
| Acquisition Rate                       | 0.1    | 0.1    | 0.1  |       | 0.1     | 0.1         |
| Creates Account                        | 10     | 20     | 34   |       | 267.856 | 357.536     |
| Total Account                          | 10     | 24     | 42   |       | 347.536 | 464.6784    |
| Activation Rate                        | 0.4    | 0.4    | 0.4  |       | 0.4     | 0.4         |
| Articles Read                          | 4      | 4      | 4    |       | 4       | 4           |
| Avg. Articles Shared                   | 2      | 2      | 2    |       | 2       | 2           |
| Avg Views Per Article                  | 5      | 5      | 5    |       | 5       | 5           |
| Referrals Per Week                     | 10     | 10     | 10   |       | 10      | 10          |
| % of new Accounts that become paid     | 0.33   | 0.33   | 0.33 |       | 0.33    | 0.33        |
| Total Paid Accounts                    | 4      | 10     | 17   |       | 55      | 186         |
| Retention Rate                         | 0.99   | 0.99   | 0.99 |       | 0.99    | 0.99        |
| Avg. Advertising Revenue/ Free User    | $0.01  | $0.01  | $0.01 |      | $0.01   | $0.01       |
| Avg. Revenue/Paid User                 | $9     | $9     | $9   |       | $9      | $9          |
| New Revenue                            | $36    | $180   | $180 |       | $2,411  | $3,217.82   |
| Recurring Revenue                      | 0      | 0      | 0    |       | 0       | 0           |
| Total Weekly Revenue                   | $36    | $180   | $306 |       | $2,411  | $3,218      |
| Monthly Run Rate                       | $144   | $720   | $1,224 |     | $9,643  | $12,871.30  |
|                                        |        |        |      |       |         | $4,182.11   |

only a fixed number per month. We might aim for a higher activation rate, but that would only raise the monthly run rate in a linear fashion. Raise the acquisition rate, though, and the run rate jumps exponentially. Doubling customer acquisition from 10 percent to 20 percent yields a run rate of $679,350—not bad.

Now we know that the acquisition rate is critical to success. We'll devote the first round of product revisions to achieving that metric. It's time to do whatever we can to increase the chance that people will sign up: Make registration as easy as possible, tinker with the registration page copy, present testimonials, offer a gift for signing up, and make the service as enticing as possible to people who receive shared articles.

At this point, we're ready to release the product and start gathering real-world measurements. By watching how the metrics trend, we can determine which are most critical to success. In the first week or two, we might find that the upgrade percentage isn't 33.3 percent but only 10 percent. We learn from further customer interviews that people are more likely to upgrade if they can try the pro version for free. So we develop a feature that lets users enter a credit card number, try it free for the first month, and pay an automatic charge unless they cancel.

| | 1 | 2 | 3 | . . . | 9 | 10 |
|---|---|---|---|---|---|---|
| Impressions from media properties (weekly) | 100 | 100 | 100 | | 100 | 100 |
| Recurring Referral Traffic | 0 | 0 | 0 | | 0 | 0 |
| New Referral Traffic | 0 | 200 | 680 | | 137533.76 | 322263.36 |
| Promotion Traffic | 0 | 0 | 0 | | 0 | 0 |
| Total Traffic | 100 | 300 | 780 | | 137634 | 322363 |
| Acquisition Rate | 0.2 | 0.2 | 0.2 | | 0.2 | 0.2 |
| Creates Account | 20 | 60 | 156 | | 27526.752 | 64472.672 |
| Total Account | 20 | 68 | 180 | | 32226.336 | 75483.3728 |
| Activation Rate | 0.4 | 0.4 | 0.4 | | 0.4 | 0.4 |
| Articles Read | 4 | 4 | 4 | | 4 | 4 |
| Avg. Articles Shared | 2 | 2 | 2 | | 2 | 2 |
| Avg Views Per Article | 5 | 5 | 5 | | 5 | 5 |
| Referrals Per Week | 10 | 10 | 10 | | 10 | 10 |
| % of new Accounts that become paid | 0.33 | 0.33 | 0.33 | | 0.33 | 0.33 |
| Total Paid Accounts | 8 | 27 | 72 | | 12891 | 30193 |
| Retention Rate | 0.99 | 0.99 | 0.99 | | 0.99 | 0.99 |
| Avg. Advertising Revenue/ Free User | $0.01 | $0.01 | $0.01 | | $0.01 | $0.01 |
| Avg. Revenue/Paid User | 9 | $9 | $9 | | $9 | $9 |
| New Revenue | $72 | $540 | $1,404 | | $247,741 | $580,254.05 |
| Recurring Revenue | $72 | 0 | 0 | | 0 | 0 |
| Total Weekly Revenue | $286 | $540 | $1,404 | | $247,741 | $580,254 |
| Monthly Run Rate | 0 | $2,160 | $5,616 | | $990,963 | $2,321,016.19 $679,350.36 |

In further tests, that brings the upgrade rate up to 25 percent. We're trading revenue for sign-ups in the short run, but we're still converting a large percentage of the user base to the paid plan. We might try making up the revenue by putting more ads in the free version and see whether that has positive effect on upgrades or a negative effect on retention.

How long should we persevere? The answer depends on both the business's performance in the real world and lessons learned from past experience. We've spent one week interviewing customers and validating the concept with a landing page, two weeks concierging, one week wireframing and creating a metrics model, and two to six weeks designing and developing the minimum feature set. Once the product is live, we'll spend another four to eight weeks of real-world operation fine-tuning the product. Assuming that every sign along the way is positive, we might spend 12 to 18 weeks to get an app to product/market fit.

By choosing appropriate metrics, modeling, and experimenting with prototypes, we can get a clear sense of how our business is likely to perform in the real world. This takes a lot of the uncertainty out of innovating and helps us direct our resources toward winning ideas before the losers can eat up the budget.

### *Case Study: Learnist, Farbood Nivi, Cofounder*

Farbood Nivi is an expert on lean startup metrics. Eric Ries featured his online social standardized test–prep company Grokit in his book's chapter on that topic. Nivi sold the Grokit name to Kaplan in July 2013, and since then, he has focused full time on Learnist, an online service that delivers crowd-sourced, crowdcurated educational ebooks. Learnist entered private beta in May 2012 and launched its first mobile app three months later. Fueled by $20 million from Discovery, Summit, Atlas, Benchmark, and others, the service reached 1 million users in late 2013. Nivi took time out to explain how he's using metrics to capture the next million.

### *What's Your Personal Approach to Innovation?*

I have a history of making fun of the word innovation. It's a word that people have said over and over until you can't really hear it anymore. I'm not even sure what it means.

### *How About Your Approach to Product Development?*

I have two. One is a gut approach: Wouldn't it be cool if you could do this? A lot of ideas come out of that question. The other is to suss out whether an idea just sounds cool or whether it actually could be cool: Does it solve a problem? What is the problem? Who has that problem? And, most important, how big a problem is it? I firmly believe that I have an infinite number of problems, and I won't solve 99.9 percent of them in my lifetime. So the real question is, is this problem big enough that someone is going to do something about it? If you build a product only because it solves a problem, you're 99.9 percent likely to fail, if only because most people don't try to solve 99.9 percent of their problems. They don't have time to deal with all their problems, so they pick off the most important ones.

### *What's Your Approach to Metrics?*

We've been hardcore into metrics for years, constantly learning, changing, fine-tuning. There are macro-level metrics that are important to the business, and once you dial in on them, they won't change much. Those are the ones you use to make business decisions. Then there are metrics related to specific features you're building. You use them to get a sense of how, where, and when those features are being used. Those metrics change as you add, subtract, and revise features. You need to watch both kinds. Also, I believe it's important to have a dedicated metrics person. If your team includes only two to four people, you probably won't have one. But if a corporation is trying to implement the lean startup method and you have 15 or 20 people, one of them ought to be a full-time data person. That person doesn't need to have a PhD in computer science, but you need someone working on data full time, working with the stakeholders to set up instrumentation and reporting so you can tell whether what you're doing is going anywhere.

### *How Do You Pick the Right Ones?*

Finding the metrics that are important for your business is a discovery process. In the end, it has to do with your business model. You may be building a cool app and feeling like, "Let's see if we can get a few million users and then figure it out as a business model." In that case, you're just trying to get a few million monthly users, so there's just one number. Maybe you want to build an advertising-based business. Then monthly users aren't important but page views are. Start by looking at the numbers that are relevant to comparable businesses in the market, and in your market in general. At some point, you'll need to attract investors or sell the business. What metrics do investors or acquirers find relevant in your industry? If

*(Continued)*

(*Continued*)

you're an ad-based business and you talk about the number of monthly users, the market might not understand: "We don't care. We want to know how many *page views* those users are consuming each month. Then we can tell whether you have a good business." The metrics associated with specific features give you the information you need to make those features work the way you want them to. You might think a particular feature should move the needle on one of the macro metrics that are basic to your business, but it doesn't. That doesn't mean you should abandon that feature. You need to look at the metrics around it, because maybe you can fix it so that it will have the right effect on the macro metric. Sometimes a feature does well in its own right, but overall it has a detrimental effect on the macro metrics that matter to the business. If you're just tracking metrics associated with features, you might get a lot of usage, but you won't improve the business. But if you're only watching the macro metrics, you might not understand why a feature that should have an effect isn't working.

### *What Are the Fundamental Metrics at Learnist?*

There are a just handful of things we really care about: month-over-month retention rate; page views, returning user rate, which is tied to month–over–month retention and the number of times an average user uses it in a month. We build features designed to move the needle on those things, launch it, and see whether it works. One hypothesis was that if people had access to more fresh content, they'd engage more with the app and improve the retention rate. So we built a feed-like experience, released it, and watched. We saw a really big improvement. Then we saw it flatten out. Now we're looking at what we learned from that experiment, as well as other data, and we're rolling that into our next sprint. We've grown 20 times since this time last year, so we feel good, pushing a couple of million active monthlies. Now we have to do it again.

### How Did You Decide on Your Fundamental Metrics?

First we got our assumptions down. What handful of things must occur for this business to be successful? Then we picked a metric to reflect each assumption and instrument to make sure I'm getting that data. We instrumented it, threw the app out there, and got a baseline for each number. From there, we modeled out the business to see whether the data points would result in a scalable business. We built a dashboard that has each of the assumptions written in English, and next to each the metric we're tracking, and that feeds a model of the business.

### Tell Us About the Dashboard

We built a pretty simple dashboard because we've built complicated ones in the past. You've got to keep things simple. I can't stress that enough. The overhead of building good instrumentation can crush your ability to get good metrics. We've gone from rolling a lot of our own tools to using as much off-the-shelf stuff as we possibly can.

### How Can Focusing on Instrumentation Crush Your Ability to Get Good Metrics?

When you roll your own instrumentation, you're building another product, which requires resources that could be devoted to the product. Instead, they're devoted to making a chart to show you metrics. Depending on the size of your team and the amount of data you're gathering, it can slow things down. You're trying to build Instagram, but you're also building an instrumentation product, and trying to do too much at

(Continued)

(*Continued*)

once is the kiss of death of a small organization. You don't realize it's happening. Suddenly it's, "We're building two products and neither is getting done." I have a quantum physicist doing my data analytics, but I'd rather him spend his time making meaning out of data than writing code to do instrumentation. We go through periods where it seems like the instrumentation is three weeks behind the product, but worrying about that is pointless. We can still look at data a couple weeks later; it's not the end of the world. The salient point is to try to match the speed of your ability to instrument and your ability to develop new features.

### What Tools Do You Use?

We're super hardcore instrumented in Google Analytics, and I recommend that people put a lot of energy into getting good at using it. If Google Analytics can't provide the information you need, then I wonder whether you're looking for the right info. We also use Chartio. It lets you mash up your own data with Google Analytics to produce charts that we use to educate other stakeholders in the organization. We've built a nice split-testing infrastructure. We use a combination of our own code and third-party stuff that makes it easy to run split tests and get reporting back.

### Do You Recall a Pivot-or-Persevere Moment When Metrics Made the Difference?

The biggest thing for us was looking at return rate. We wanted to see whether we could get people to return without spending money. It doesn't seem like a serviceable business if the organic return rate isn't over 30 percent pretty early. I think about it in terms of trying to double that number. If you go from 5 to 10 percent or 10 to 20 percent, you're not accomplishing much. But if you can go from 30 to 60 percent, that's great. So it was a major milestone when we got to 30 percent.

### *Did You Consider That Point Product/Market Fit?*

It depends on your definition. Anything early-stage is the netting out of the team, idea, and market. To the extent that there's enough alignment between two of those three, the market, including employees, investors, and so on, will probably be interested in seeing what can come of this. Eventually you reach the point where the players involved feel that the unknowns are worth exploring because the potential rewards are very high.

### *How Do You Define Product/Market Fit?*

Some people say you'll know when you get there. That's like saying you'll know you're rich when you have a billion dollars. I want to know when I'm trending toward becoming rich. So it's not useful to say that product/market fit is when a product is growing like crazy. What's useful is knowing when you're close enough that it's worth going on, or you're so far away that it's pointless to continue.

### *How Do You Avoid Vanity Metrics and Keep the Focus on Actionable Metrics?*

A vanity metric can become a relevant metric. Page views is a great example. That's something I ignored until recently because it was a pure vanity metric. But now that we're looking at the business as potential ad-driven, page views is a very useful metric. I can model potential revenue based on it. So one day it was a vanity metric; the next day it's the most important one. You need to have the intellectual honesty with yourself and your team to ask, "Which metrics are relevant to our business?" All others are vanity.

### *How Does a Project's Engine of Growth Affect Your Choice of Metrics?*

It's a useful framework for thinking about what to do. That's a starting point, and your metrics should match what you're doing.

*(Continued)*

(*Continued*)

### At What Point in a Project Do You Start Modeling?

If it's a direct purchase business, I always start with a model. If I'm selling, say, jet engines, I'm looking at how many engines I need to sell a year, at what price, and much it costs to build one. If it's a consumer media property that's based on usage, I build a product first. A model won't be useful for telling me whether I have 20 million or 30 million active monthly users, and I just focus on scaling up. Once I have baseline metrics, then I build a specific and sophisticated model of the business that is informed by those baselines, my assumptions about how to get to 20 million active users, and tests that help me determine user acquisition costs and per-user revenue.

### What Features Have You Added That Had the Greatest Impact?

Search engine optimization. I didn't expect that. SEO had a lot to do with our 20-times growth over the past year. You have to study how the search engines are looking at you. The search engines provide tools to do that, and there are other tools as well. They'll point out problem areas that make your site difficult for Google to see, and if you fix them, you'll rise in the search rankings if Google finds your pages relevant. It goes beyond optimizing single pages. You can tell Google about how the information is organized and provide additional forms of metadata. Most developers don't think along that line, so frequently you'll get a website that Google can't read well. Between 30 and 50 percent of our traffic comes from SEO. That was one of the big learnings early on, and it focused us on other questions: What percentage is mobile? What percentage is organic versus referral versus direct? Is 30 to 50 percent the maximum? Can we get more? Asking those questions and having good ways to answer them is extremely helpful.

# Chapter 9

# Incubate Internally

Of the three enterprise innovation strategies—incubating, investing, and acquiring—incubating internally is the hardest. You're creating something out of nothing: You're on the hook for brilliant ideas. Moreover, your startups begin with zero momentum, and you're responsible for bringing them to fruition by using internal resources. They might have to compete for internal resources, or even with products that are the company's bread and butter.

Maybe that's why enterprises have proven so bad at incubation. Take Microsoft. The company that built an industry around MS-DOS and then Windows is no slouch at innovation, yet even the monarch of the desktop operating system wasn't able to generate success with two major internal projects, Zune and Surface. (On the other hand, Xbox is a striking counterpoint, and a very successful one at that.)

Zune was a notorious failure. The purported iPod killer, launched in 2006 five years after Apple's wildly successful music player, generated

$117 million in revenue during Q4 2008 compared to iPod's $3.37 billion around the same time. Microsoft finally laid it to rest in 2012.

Perhaps it's too soon to be sure about Surface, but early indications don't look good. In July 2013, the company slashed prices and announced a $900 million charge on the device, equivalent to a loss of $0.07 per share. Incidentally, neither product was a disruptive innovation; both were me-too follow-ups to Apple's success.

Incubating disruptive products goes against the grain of older, larger companies. It requires creativity, flexibility, collaboration, and speed, qualities that dissipate as a company grows out of disrupting its initial competitors and settles into nurturing and protecting its existing lines of business. The enterprise employees we work with have a hard time thinking beyond the confines of their departmental functions and an even harder time acting independently. They tend to solve low-level problems that have little impact on the bottom line, problems that customers might not even notice. It doesn't occur to them to think in terms of redefining their industry, and if they did, the corporate silos and hierarchy wouldn't allow it.

A large financial institution we coached exhibited the kind of myopia that we encounter every day. The product development team insisted on boosting its credit card customers' use of rewards and other benefits despite lack of any evidence that such an increase would improve its business. The team members wanted to work on a portal that would further this aim, although they had no reason to believe that customers would use it. This, in an industry that's being redefined by dozens of upstarts from Google Wallet to Dwolla to Bitcoin, all of which anticipate multibillion-dollar returns. Nonetheless, the product development team couldn't remove their legacy blinders long enough to see the dizzying array of opportunities staring them in the face.

Developing the capacity to conceive, develop, and sell products beyond the company's existing business units is vital if enterprises hope to thrive in an increasingly fast-moving, hypercompetitive, and hyperconnected business environment. For mature companies, the path to high growth leads inevitably through the realm of high uncertainty. The higher the uncertainty, the higher the return on learning and, eventually, return on investment.

## Low Momentum, High Control

Incubating internally offers the lowest momentum of the three enterprise innovation strategies. As opposed to investing in a business that's already growing or acquiring a startup that's well on its way to product/market fit, you're starting from a whiteboard. That said, there's no reason why startups incubated internally can't explode into the market and grow faster and bigger than investments or acquisitions. They just take more effort to get off the ground.

At the same time, this strategy gives you the highest level of control, and face it, some executives cannot bear the thought of going without. The enterprise can retain up to 49 percent of the equity of any given project, as opposed to investing or acquiring, in which other shareholders will have carved up the shares. (Mind you, the 49 percent figure obviously doesn't favor the enterprise, but it supports the founders' sense of ownership and autonomy by making it possible for them to own a majority stake. Meanwhile, the enterprise will hold a board seat, giving it an extra measure of influence.) By taking on more risk at the beginning, you can minimize risk in the end.

Note that the line between incubating internally and investing in an external company is a fine one. The biggest differences are that the incubation team earns a salary and takes advantage of corporate resources such as workspace, infrastructure, and in-house services, and that the enterprise potentially has a greater share of ownership.

News Corp's print properties have taken this route since June 2013, when the company spun out its more lucrative entertainment business (now called 21st Century Fox). The publishing behemoth that includes the *Wall Street Journal* and the *Times of London* set aside $20 million to incubate new products from scratch (the target number is 64). It hired people with startup and product-development experience, trained them in lean startup methods, and contracted independent software shops to get the wheels moving. It remains to be seen whether the company's innovation effort can produce compelling products that transcend its legacy operations and transform its industry, but it's off to a great start.

# Benefits

Incubating internally offers benefits beyond putting your company's innovation efforts on firm footing. Of the three strategies, it's the most capital efficient. That is, you'll spend the least money over time compared to acquiring and investing. The cost to the enterprise consists mainly of salaries (at a substantial discount). As a project gains traction, it will generate revenue that supports its own growth.

Furthermore, this strategy fosters latent entrepreneurial talent within the current roster of employees, potentially boosting revenue per employee. It gives people who might leave to start their own company an incentive to stay and develop their idea at lower financial risk to themselves. And it gives people who are more risk-averse, who are more comfortable working for a salary than striking out on their own, an opportunity to develop new products and target opportunities they wouldn't otherwise take on. In short, it gives employees a powerful incentive to think and work entrepreneurially on behalf of the company.

At the same time, it gives acqui-hires an environment that will maximize their productivity. They can work on startups that benefit the enterprise without having to become corporate drones. They get to do what they're good at—creating and launching new products—with less personal financial risk than they had to accept in the startup world.

Creating innovative products from scratch benefits the enterprise as a whole by making all your employees feel innovative. It confers a sense of pride and passion that business as usual can't. Cranking out forward-looking projects can be a powerful morale booster throughout the company.

# Financing Internal Startups

It's impossible to put a rational value on seed-stage startups, so it's helpful to look at what other organizations do. Techstars offers roughly $20,000 in return for 6 percent of ownership in companies it incubates. That figure amounts to a valuation of $333,000 per company, which can be viewed as a sensible floor. After all, if you offer less, your teams will be justified in fleeing to Techstars. We suggest an equally arbitrary valuation of at least $500,000 per startup—though the more capital you offer, the more serious entrepreneurs you'll attract.

If the colony funds 49 percent of an internal startup at a valuation of $500,000, the team will have $240,000 for its initial runway. Divided between three founders as an annual salary, the runway will last a year. Thrifty founders can make it last longer. During that time, the innovation team experiments constantly to develop a combination of features and capabilities that attracts and retains a critical mass of customers. At some point, though, the money will run out. If, by that time, the startup's value is deemed to be growing, the team might sell further equity to the enterprise and keep going. Alternatively, the enterprise and/or team might sell a portion to outside investors to keep the startup alive. If the startup has reached product/market fit but the enterprise takes a pass, the team can spin it off as an independent company and leave the innovation colony.

Otherwise, the startup has run its course. The incubator shuts it down and the team moves on to another project. Those who are discouraged can leave the colony and move into other positions within the enterprise. Those who stay on will be smarter innovators for the experience.

## How to Incubate

The key to productive incubation is to embrace lean startup methods wholeheartedly. This approach, which we cover in depth in Lean Enterprise Process (Chapter 6), provides a disciplined process for measuring the progress of new ideas from concept to product/market fit. Where developing new products and bringing them to market once was a hit-or-miss proposition, techniques such as customer development, minimum viable products, and innovation accounting offer a way to validate new ideas and develop them into offerings that large numbers of customers will pay for.

You'll want to employ as many innovation teams as your budget allows, each focused on a project that's aligned with your innovation hypothesis. (See Innovation Flow (Chapter 12) for a sense of how budgeting relates to team size.) Speed is essential so, at the beginning at least, don't take on ideas for which a minimum viable product can't be built within three months.

In addition, consider bringing an entrepreneur in residence. This is a way to recruit talented people who wouldn't otherwise consider joining an enterprise, and it can broaden your network by connecting the innovation colony to the wider startup community. The entrepreneur in residence isn't formally employed by the colony. Instead, this person comes in for a residency of six months or one year, with an option to extend—enough time to pursue a project of mutual interest. Like members of the innovation teams, an entrepreneur in residence takes a significant portion of the upside in startups under his or her direction.

Don't be afraid to shut down projects that don't show immediate promise. The innovation teams should be pivoting constantly until a project begins to develop momentum, but after dozens of pivots, some concepts will reveal themselves not to be worth pursuing. Killing them is a good outcome; it avoids wasting time and resources on ideas you've vetted thoroughly and concluded aren't worth the effort.

### Generating Ideas

Great businesses are based on great ideas. However, the incubator doesn't start with great ideas—it starts with plain, unproven ideas and then uses lean startup techniques to develop them into ones that can sustain a business. So it needs a steady supply of raw material to work on.

Where do these ideas come from? Part of the answer is the broad network of accelerators, funders, and entrepreneurs that the incubation colony cultivates over time. This milieu keeps the managing directors in touch with developments in the startup community that can spur creative thinking. Over time, the directors will tune their antennae to ideas that have breakout potential.

Beyond that, great ideas arise from inspiration. A personal experience may call attention to a problem that needs solving. Conversations with friends and acquaintances can reveal hidden needs. A news article may spark a thought about how things might work differently. Everyone involved with the colony should be on the lookout for ideas.

In the interest of capturing as many of those concepts as possible, the incubator should have an open policy for anyone who wants to submit a proposal. Employees of the enterprise at large should be free to pitch a hypothesis at any time. If it's accepted, they can move to the incubator to develop the idea.

Some companies spur employees to come up with new ideas by offering so-called 20 percent time. However, we believe that an open door to the corporate incubator with a promise of sharing in the upside gives workers a far greater incentive. Google, for instance, famously encourages employees to spend one-fifth of their working hours pursuing an idea of personal interest. Some of these projects become products, and those that achieve extraordinary success are eligible to win a prize of shares in the company. Take Gmail: Engineer Paul Buchheit started it in the early 2000s as a 20 percent project, developed it into a flagship product, launched the beta version in 2004, and won a Founder's Award in late 2007. But what if Buchheit had been able to bring Gmail to an incubator with the knowledge that he would share in the upside? Admittedly this is a wild-ass speculation, but we think it's likely that Paul would have been even more motivated to develop the product, and it would have reached the market years earlier.

You can also spur new ideas by running an inspiration program. Among the most powerful tools in this regard are Lean Startup Machine workshops and hackathons. These events can be a lot of fun for participants. For the incubator, they generate raw material and attract entrepreneurial talent.

A Lean Startup Machine workshop is an intensive group exercise that concentrates on discovering an unmet customer need and validating a solution. It provides intensive training in lean startup-style experimentation, and it's a fantastic way to fill the funnel of ideas.

A hackathon is a similar type of program focused on building new products in the course of the event itself. It's great for developing technical skills and strengthening team cohesion, and it often results in useable products. Between the two, you can generate large numbers of ideas very quickly, gain solid evidence of how the market may greet them, and generate viable products. In fact, corporate IT departments frequently use hackathons to develop software products for internal use.

You can hold Lean Startup Machines and hackathons on a quarterly basis, so employees get into the habit of dreaming up ideas in anticipation. The events will draw employees from other departments, generating interest in the innovation colony and attracting people who have the ambition and temperament to make good innovation team members. You can also invite independent entrepreneurs, engineers, marketers, designers, and other interested parties in your community. That way, your idea-generation activities will build your network as well.

### Organizing a Lean Startup Machine

A Lean Startup Machine (LSM) workshop generally unfolds over two days. The goal is to validate or invalidate hypotheses in the shortest possible time. The winner isn't the team that produces the most interesting or impressive product but the one that accomplishes the most learning about what customers want and how to give it to them.

The basic requirements for a Lean Startup Machine event include a venue, food (pizza and sodas are fine; you need something that people can eat without interrupting their activities), and access to customers. This last item is crucial; participants need to be able to find real-world customers, whether by soliciting on the street, sending e-mail, posting a Facebook page, or making phone calls. You'll also need a leader and mentors who are familiar with the format. After you've staged a few of these events, former participants can play those roles. In addition to helping teams to focus their efforts, the mentors can give presentations teaching basic lean startup skills: how to find customers, how to interview them, how to build a minimum viable product, how to sell a product before it's available. All that's left is to gather everyone together, state the rules, and unleash the group's creativity and ingenuity.

LSM teams form around an idea for a marketable product or service. Our own Javelin Board can guide them through the process (see Chapter 6). They'll perform a series of experiments and, after each one, make a decision to pivot or persevere. The aim is to develop a minimum viable product that has paying customers (or customers who have committed to pay) before time runs out.

At the end of two days, the participants present their work and describe what they learned. Then the organizers and mentors pick winners based on which teams achieved the greatest learning. The prizes can be just about anything; lunch with the CEO is a good motivator. It's also a good idea to advertise the first-place team widely throughout the company to generate interest and amplify competitive spirit.

## *How to Run a Hackathon*

Like an LSM, a hackathon usually takes place over two full days, although the format can work in a single day. Many of the requirements are the same: venue, food, mentors, leader, prizes. Participants form teams around ideas—anything goes; projects can range from serious product concepts to whimsical Rube Goldberg machines—and then get to work transforming them into functional products as quickly as possible. When the time is up, the teams present their projects. Then the organizers and mentors pick a winner based on the best execution.

---

**Inspiration in Action**

TLC makes software for libraries, including public and academic libraries worldwide. (The initials stand for "The Library Company.") Founded in 1974, TLC has its headquarters in Linwood, West Virginia, and offices in Denver, New York, and Singapore. With 300 employees, it doesn't qualify as an enterprise. However, it's a mature company with significant market share in a contracting market. More to the point, TLC is using lean enterprise incubation techniques to create new products and discover new markets.

TLC's flagship products are innovative within the library space, but its approach to product development has never focused on innovation. But 40 TLC employees took part in a Lean Startup Machine workshop in early 2012. Within six months, the company was hosting its own workshops and hackathons. These events yielded three projects that were earmarked for further development, and the company set up an innovation lab in its New York office. One of them, eBibliofile, generated substantial business in its first month. Two customers signed up for annual plans, yielding a $1 million run rate right out of the gate.

*(Continued)*

(*Continued*)

TLC's lab began with a thesis so broad that it was closer to a theme: software for mobile devices, with an emphasis on the iPad. Participation is open to any employee who wants to take part. The company invites workers to submit ideas and offers a week away from regular responsibilities to develop the most promising ones.

As an added incentive, any project that receives a mention on the TechCrunch news site immediately earns an extra measure of ownership for the team members who developed it. This "buzzworthiness incentive" is designed to motivate not only the innovation teams, but employees throughout the company. TLC is an old company in a dying business, and a mention in the premier tech blog would energize the entire operation and prompt the public at large to view the company in a new, more innovative light.

TLC's experience shows that an old-line company with little or no innovation experience can create valuable new lines of business from scratch given appropriate structures, incentives, and activities. The task of turning inspirations into money-making products isn't easy, but it's eminently achievable within a lean enterprise setting.

### Case Study: News Corp, Nick Bell, SVP Digital Products

With market-leading news outlets in the United Kingdom, United States, and Australia, News Corp—which split off from 21st Century Fox in June 2013—is one of the world's media heavyweights. Not only does it manage centuries-old properties such as the *Times* of London, it spins out new products at a prodigious rate, thanks to Nick Bell. Based in Manhattan, Bell and his six-person innovation team expands the company's core businesses by looking for opportunities throughout the

News Corp universe and beyond, launching new products as far afield as Southeast Asia. Bell spoke with us about how his team incubates both incremental and disruptive innovations.

### How Did You Arrive in Your Current Position?

I had an unconventional route into the corporate world. I built a website, teenfront.com, in my bedroom in 1998, when I was 14, and sold it at 16 at the height of the dot-com boom. I continued to build and grow businesses for another 10 years before joining News International, which is News Corp's U.K. subsidiary. I ran digital there for two and a half years before being asked to join the headquarters team, which I did in May 2013.

### What's Your Personal Approach to Innovation?

First, it's important to have a sense of disruption. When I first created a website back in the early days, I thought anything was possible, because I didn't have a sense of what wasn't. When I first joined News International, I went in and asked, "Why do we do it that way?" It's important to bring in people with a fresh outlook and pair them with people who have a huge amount of experience to get that natural tension going.

The second part is having a very clear focus on the customer from day one. You need to ask: How will they use it? How does it fit into their schedule? How does it change their daily life? You need to identify people who can help you answer these questions. Large organizations are guilty of building it and expecting customers to come, particularly in a corporation like News Corp, where we touch hundreds of millions of people every day. It's easy to get reach and scale, but that doesn't necessarily mean it's long-term reach and scale or truly engaged reach and scale. It's vital to get the product into people's hands early and get their feedback as soon as possible.

*(Continued)*

*(Continued)*

### There's a Perception That Enterprises Are Bad at Incubation. Why Is That?

I always say that News Corp has five major assets: reach and scale to address hundreds of millions of people a day, the best-quality content in the world, our 30,000 talented people, a huge amount of data, and a lot of cash. But these assets are also our biggest challenges. Our reach and scale makes us risk-averse to launch new products that might tarnish our brand. Having a large amount of content means we can enter different verticals, but sometimes it's difficult to decide which one. Having 30,000 employees can make us slow-moving, because that's a lot of minds to align. We have so much data that it's easy to waste a lot of time overanalyzing things. And finally, if we're not careful with our money we could spend too much.

### How Do You Keep Those Assets from Becoming Weaknesses?

We've taken major steps to avoid falling into the traps I just mentioned. We're lucky within News Corp, actually, because the business headquarters is small and nimble. There are 20 to 30 people involved in the strategy, creative, and technology teams. So getting decisions made is easy and deciding to change culture is easy. We work very closely and know each other inside out. And we're careful about the people we put on projects. We have a core team made up of people who have come out of startups, and I'm mixing them up with people who have been with the company for years, creating natural friction and diversity. So far, that has been pretty successful.

### Can You Give Us a Sense of the Scope of Your Incubation Projects?

First, we're repurposing content. If you look at the Internet, content is the most expensive piece of the mix. We have a huge amount of it, so one of the biggest opportunities is to create the long tail for it. We have a lot of evergreen content—recipes, tutorials, product reviews, movie reviews, music reviews—but we don't exploit it very well at the moment. The second part is attracting a younger audience. Newspapers tend to skew to an older demographic. The average age of our readers is 50-plus, so we're looking for ways to target a younger audience.

### Is There a Difference Between Incubating Incremental versus Disruptive Innovations?

We're trying to do a combination of both. We tend to be more incremental in our approach to existing businesses, and we tend to be more radical and disruptive when we're launching new business. But even with the new businesses we launch, there's always a parallel path of financial gain and knowledge. Commercial success is important, but we also want to apply the learnings back into our existing business.

### How Do You Generate Ideas for Incubation? How Do You Vet Them?

We're still experimenting to find the best way to do that. At the moment, anyone in the business can bubble up an idea. We hold exploration workshops around different topics or customer segments. If the topic is food, for instance, we'll bring in food experts from London, Australia, and New York, mix them with our innovation teams, come up with a few ideas, and build them out to a level where they can be tested in the market. Then we'll decide whether to invest further.

### How Do Ideas Develop from There?

There are a few ways that can go. If we think there's more work to do, we do research. If we feel there's potentially a new

*(Continued)*

*(Continued)*

business, someone will be assigned to drive it full time until they validate or invalidate it. If it looks like a good opportunity for an existing business unit, we'll talk to that business unit about how to adopt it into their current product or feature set. We may think it has strategy change potential. Our global ad exchange came out of an advertising workshop. Or it may lead to an acquisition. During the workshop, we'll explore competitors, and companies may bubble up that prompt an early conversation on due diligence.

### How Many Projects Do You Have in Motion at Any Given Time?

Probably four or five, but it depends on the size. Some stuff we've done ended up being absorbed or adopted by existing business units. When that happens, we like to stay involved and make sure they're on the right path.

### How Do You Fund Incubator Projects? Is an Initial Allocation Used to Establish a Runway?

We have a central pot; we haven't disclosed the amount, but it's a significant budget. We don't ask the existing business units to fund an idea out of their P&L until we've validated it. The cost is certainly not free, but it's not billed and assigned. On the other hand, we've been careful to put in place a strict governance process, so we don't just throw cash at problems. To get more cash, you need to hit certain success criteria. That creates a real discipline around getting traction or pivoting until we meet those success criteria, rather than throwing good money after bad.

### What Is the Average Schedule and Budget for Incubating a Project?

It varies a great deal. One of the key things we're trying to work through here is failing fast. There have been times when we've run an exploration and felt we had the bases covered, or it was too early or too late, or the market was too small or wasn't the right fit for us. In those instances, after two weeks we decide not to pursue it. As for investment, some things are done internally without spending any money apart from the core team. The five of us get together and come up with some ideas. Then, alongside our day jobs, we speak with customers and create a prototype. Then it might be four or five weeks before we have feedback on the prototype.

### What Role Does the Lean Startup Method Play?

We don't follow it religiously, but we do follow the underlying ethos of driving to market quickly, testing, and validating a concept before spending too much money. The lean startup method works for us on the innovation team, but our existing business units find it trickier to implement. They especially struggle with the brand issue. The News Corp brand can help make a new product successful, because we have the credibility and the user base, but often we're concerned about taking the product to market in case we don't launch or it damages our reputation. That said, we have created a number of test tools or platforms. In the U.K., they've launched Tea with the *Times*, a weekly event where they invite in existing customers and float ideas and prototypes. Because they do these things regularly, they don't mind testing a paper sketch rather than waiting until they've built something more refined and polished.

### What Percentage of Projects Makes It to the Prototype Stage? To the Product Stage?

All of them make it to prototype. Sixty to 70 percent will make it to a further stage of adoption, whether it's research or learnings that circulate to the wider business and impact future

*(Continued)*

*(Continued)*

products or features, or whether it's a feature built into a future product. Ten percent make it to product stage.

### Don't Some Ideas Fail Before They Reach Prototype?

There tends to be a huge amount of pivoting over the course of early exploration, but usually the output is a prototype that represents the best of those sessions. We're mixing people from outside the incubation team with the incubation team, and I think it's good to take people through the whole cycle. We're not just validating an idea but trying to create a culture that people can take back into our existing business units.

### What Is Your Success Criteria?

From the early exploration sessions, there's usually some form of validation from customers, whether it's just people telling us to carry on, or sign-ups, or even hard cash. The key thing is to set explicit criteria early on, so we don't find ourselves in the situation where a project continues because people say, "It hasn't quite worked, but it's going okay." That gives us the discipline to acknowledge failure. We don't necessarily kill the project, but it means we need to pivot or explain the steps that will take us to the next set of success criteria.

### How Do You Evaluate Return on Investment?

Every project has to return commercially and financially within a period of time, and that's agreed with the CSO and the team prior to going into a project. But softer elements are also important, such as experience or learnings.

### How Many Projects Do You Have to Incubate to Score a Hit?

We don't have a clear view of that yet. Out of 10, we'd be lucky to have two or three successes and another five or six that move on in some form.

### *What's Your Proudest Success?*

Recently, we launched a soccer app called BallBall into Indonesia, Vietnam, and Japan. The idea was conceived and launched in eight weeks, going into a new territory on Android, iPhone, and a responsive-design website—that was something this business has never seen. The product checks three boxes for us. It's a new territory, Southeast Asia, where we don't have a particularly strong foothold; it's aimed at a youth audience; and it reuses content that we already produce. The key was to do it lean and mean, get it into the market as quickly as possible, and to start learning from customers.

# Chapter 10

# Acquire Early

Whether you incubate new products and services from within your enterprise, acquisition is another important tool in the lean enterprise kit. Purchasing a startup can buy you products and services that you don't have the capacity or speed to develop yourself, not to mention cutting-edge technology that can rocket the enterprise ahead of competitors and provide an entrée into new markets. It can bring in people who possess an entrepreneurial spirit so often missing at businesses that have grown and matured. Better yet, those people arrive already organized into teams that have a track record of working well together, ready to be deployed toward your company's priorities. Moreover, a purchase can bring in (at least for awhile) independent-minded talent who wouldn't otherwise dream of working for a large organization like yours.

# Who Are You Looking For?

The typical enterprise acquisition is geared toward buying a company and integrating it into an existing business unit or scrapping it for talent or technology. The thinking is that the enterprise can leverage its considerable strengths in favor of the acquired company. After all, the enterprise's advantages come from its distribution channels, painstakingly developed over decades; its marketing expertise, honed through intensive experience serving a particular sort of customers; and its sterling brand, nurtured through enormous expenditures on advertising and product development. Put that power behind the acquisition, the theory goes, and the new line of business is bound to take off.

For better or worse, the Internet has destroyed the rationale behind this line of thinking. First, by the time a startup is on a steady course, it will be all over blogs, discussion boards, social networks, and news sites. Other potential acquirers will already be in line, and they will have bid up the price well beyond what makes sense if your goal is to spur innovation, which requires making a number of small bets rather than one big one.

What may be less obvious from an enterprise point of view is that a large company's strengths don't pack the punch they used to. In a networked world, distribution is a commodity. A search engine like Google is the great leveler: Customers can easily find a web page that offers access to the product they're looking for, whether it's on Amazon for hard goods, Apple's App Store or Google Play for mobile software, iTunes for music, Netflix for movies, and so on right down to the manufacturer's or publisher's own site. Meanwhile, social networking sites, especially Facebook, Twitter, and LinkedIn, have become an important means by which customers segment themselves into groups and determine what they want to buy; traditional marketing and advertising methods are crude, slow, and costly by comparison. As for the enterprise's vaunted brand, the one-two punch of search and social media have sapped it of much of its power. A brand that neither shows up in the first few search results nor garners recognition within an online community is irrelevant. Conversely, those that do—Airbnb, Angry Birds, Dropbox, Facebook, GroupOn, Pinterest, Spotify, Uber—can become powerful brands within a very short time.

So forget about acquiring a proven business that you can hitch to your enterprise's distribution, marketing, and branding apparatus. You're looking for something else. One goal is to *find unproven businesses* that fit your innovation thesis and *let them grow organically*. The other is to find established teams that you can buy to work on your own startups (known as acqui-hires).

You still need to vet acquisitions carefully, analyzing them for the characteristics most likely to lead to high growth. And you need a safe harbor—the innovation colony—where early-stage ventures can grow free of the financial and political pressures that often hobble established business units. Ideally, startups you acquire for both their products and their teams will keep their pre-acquisition offices and operate independently, maintaining the culture that created the value that made them an attractive target to begin with. Acqui-hires are likely to join your innovation colony.

Some of your acquisitions will fail. But the ones that grow will expand like mushrooms after a rain, with exponentially rising customer bases, revenues, and ultimately profits, by discovering new markets and serving them with products and services those markets truly want.

Take a look at Twitter's acquisition of mobile video app maker Vine, whose six-second time limit was something of a match for Twitter's 140-character text ceiling. The social messaging service bought the startup for $30 million in October 2012, when it was only four months old and hadn't even debuted publicly. Twitter, which is based in San Francisco, kept Vine housed in its own New York office, allowing it to run more or less autonomously. By April 2013, Vine was the most-downloaded free app in Apple's App Store, and the Android version made *Time*'s list of the year's best Android apps. As of January 2014, it had at least 40 million users.

### High Control, High Momentum

By acquiring early and nurturing the acquisition's inherent strengths, you're maximizing both control and momentum. You take full ownership with all the upside and other benefits that implies. The prospect for growth is higher than with either incubating or investing because the startup has already eliminated a degree of uncertainty, and you can exert an influence in guiding it in a way that will be most profitable within the context of your company. It's a powerful strategy that instantly makes innovation one of your company's core competencies.

## Finding Acquisition Opportunities

The trick is to identify potential high-growth opportunities ahead of competitors (who may be adversaries in your market, rival acquirers, or investors). In some ways, this isn't as difficult as it sounds. Most industry watchers follow the crowd, so by taking the initiative, you gain an automatic advantage. And frequently they don't focus on the most meaningful indicators. If you search for opportunities based on innovation accounting, you're ahead of the game.

The first move is to step into the stream of opportunities, or deal flow. Angel investors go to great pains to cultivate their deal flow, so a good place to start is to meet them and let them know what you're looking for. You can find them through AngelList, an online social network for accredited investors. Entrepreneurs look for additional funding before they consider selling, so it's a good idea to tell your angel contacts that you're interested in investing as well—this will bring into your orbit founders who might soon be ready to give up their companies. Consider bringing an experienced angel onboard to run your acquisition and/or investment program.

Seed funders, including incubators and accelerators such as 500 Startups, Techstars, and Y Combinator, also have outstanding deal flow. Forge relationships with accelerators and incubators that are active in the markets you're interested in. Attend their demo days and meet the founders who present there. Join the Global Accelerator Network, an offshoot of the Techstars accelerator that operates in 63 cities worldwide.

These organizations are likely to have in their roster startups that failed to raise early funding rounds. Such startups are at an inflection point. They've done the hard work of identifying a problem and creating a business plan around it, but they don't have the financial means to carry on. Maybe it's time to sell. So tell the executives at incubators and accelerators that you're shopping for startups and what qualities you're looking for. In all likelihood, they'll be happy to help you, if only as a way to recoup their own investment.

For that matter, any startup that's approaching the end of its runway is a viable acqui-hire. The team has learned hard lessons in what not to do, and they can bring that experience to bear in developing products on your behalf. In fact, failed startups are often acqui-hired by Facebook, Google, and other Silicon Valley giants hungry for talent. Acqui-hires outnumber straight-up acquisitions eight or nine to one on Exitround, an online marketplace that anonymously matches potential acquirers and acquisitions. Most Exitround transactions are in the $10 million to $50 million range, often involving engineering-heavy teams and enterprises in nontech industries such as hospitality or insurance that recognize the need for internal technology development, according to Exitround CEO Jacob Mullins.

And you'll want to comb through ear-to-the-ground tech publications such as TechCrunch, PandoDaily, and Hacker News and to check out new products in the App Store and Google Play. These sites can give you a heads-up on emerging opportunities that fit your innovation thesis.

Note that all these tips also go for identifying potential startups to invest in, (see Invest When You Can't Acquire (Chapter 11)) as well as finding startup-savvy talent in general. Whether you're looking to acquire, invest, or staff an internal incubation colony, you're aiming to infuse your enterprise with fresh entrepreneurial blood. These resources can help you find it.

## Choosing Acquisition Targets

The next step is to pick your targets. Opportunities are more plentiful than you might think because competitors are likely to overlook the most important factor in a successful startup: product/market fit. You're looking for a startup that suits your innovation thesis and is on the verge of achieving product/market fit, or has achieved it and doesn't yet know it.

Product/market fit, you recall, is the match between a product or service and a large base of users who want it badly enough to invest considerable time, energy, and money to use it. Prior to achieving product/market fit, a startup is a bundle of potential. Nobody really knows what it can accomplish. After achieving product/market fit, it's a freight train barreling down the track toward massive growth. Everyone involved senses gathering traction and momentum, and people around them catch on, too, including customers, competitors, investors, and the press.

By that time, the founders aren't likely to want to sell; if they do, the price is likely to be astronomical. You may want to buy anyway—you may even be able to make the founders an offer they can't refuse—but the biggest opportunity is past. So you should keep your eyes open for startups that haven't yet found a winning formula or don't yet know they have. That's when the founders will be willing to sell at a price you can afford.

It's also when you stand to reap the biggest rewards, in terms of not only upside but opportunity to dominate the market. Consider what happens when your acquisition reaches product/market fit. Customers start signing up, the social networks start buzzing, and the press jumps on the bandwagon. At that point, even fleet-footed competitors won't stand a chance of catching up. Barnes & Noble brought out its Nook ereader two years after Amazon offered the Kindle, but B&N failed to capture significant market share. BlackBerry released its PlayBook only a year after the iPad launched, but the newer device had zero impact on Apple's momentum. These days, a year is looking like a very long time as development cycles rev and new releases are ever quicker to establish their market position. By climbing aboard the rocket before it lifts off, you put yourself in a position to gain a highly defensible dominance.

How can you identify a startup on the verge of achieving product/market fit? Innovation accounting gives you a rational way to evaluate this (see Innovation Accounting (Chapter 8)). Before modeling the startup's business, though, a few subjective measures can be helpful. Ask the founders what they've learned and how they expect to scale. Try out the product and its competitors to get a clear sense of what problem it solves and how it compares. Ask customers how they use it and gauge how excited they are. Get them to take Sean Ellis's one-question survey: How disappointed would you feel if you could no longer use this product? A 40 percent "very disappointed" response is an indicator, though not a definitive qualifier, of product/market fit.

If the startup still looks promising, it's time to build a metrics model. You'll need to gather whatever metrics you can from the founders. Then design the model, plug in the existing numbers, and make conservative guesses about the ones you must make up out of thin air. Ultimately, you're looking for a demonstration that the business can acquire users profitably and thus has a clear path to scaling up.

The same principles apply to choosing investment targets (see Invest When You Can't Acquire (Chapter 11)). Whether you're investing or acquiring, you'll reap the biggest upside by choosing startups that are as close as possible to matching their product or service to a profitably scalable customer base.

## Structuring the Deal

Having settled on a startup to acquire, approach the founders and make an offer. You'll be negotiating with the founders and their investors, if any are involved. You may be tempted to try to negotiate the most favorable terms for your acquisition deals, but that's not necessarily the best approach. An enterprise environment isn't the most attractive home for an ambitious startup, and many founders will chafe at the notion of consigning their baby to a parent that might be perceived as dull-witted, lumbering, and distracted.

Your aim is not only to acquire the startup but to keep the founders productively engaged for years, possibly decades. It's common for founders to view acquisition as the end game; they won't be in charge anymore, and the best alternative is to leave and start fresh. It's up to you to change this impression. After all, the acquisition is not the end of the startup but the beginning of a new and innovative phase for the enterprise. The terms should empower and motivate the startup team and give its members a powerful incentive to stick around.

### Pricing

The price of a company with a demonstrably successful product is a complex calculation that takes into account everything from executive bonuses to buzz factor. However, you're aiming to acquire a startup that may not even have a product, much less a track record. That's a different story.

If the startup has raised an equity round, it has well-defined value, and your offer will need to meet or exceed that figure. In fact, if the startup has made arguable progress since the last equity round, you'll certainly have to pay more. For instance, Instagram was worth $500 million in March 2012, but by the time Facebook lodged its acquisition offer only one month later, the price had risen to $1 billion. Remember, companies that have reached product/market fit grow at an exponential rate—just one more reason why it's important to place your bets early.

On the other hand, you might be looking at a startup that has no momentum or has run out of cash. In this case, a nice rule of thumb is to let the investors recoup at least half their money. Let's say a startup has raised $1 million on a $4 million pre–money valuation, so it's worth $5 million by the time you arrive. An offer of $500,000 would give the investors half of what they put in. The founders themselves would get nothing, but you'd be paying them a salary (albeit a reduced one; see Compensation (Chapter 4)).

Another way to look at pricing is to consider the Silicon Valley standard for acqui-hires. The rule of thumb is $1 million to $1.5 million per engineer on the team (a formula that is likely to wax and wane with the fortunes of the Valley at large). If the startup in the example above had two engineers, then you'd offer $2 million. The investors would recoup their money in full and the common stockholders, founders, and employees would split the other $1 million.

Thus, it would be reasonable to offer between $500,000 and $2 million for the startup in our example. Keep in mind, though, that there are good reasons to lean toward the higher number. Your foremost goal should be to keep the founders fully engaged with the enterprise's innovation efforts, not to optimize the acquisition price.

### Cash versus Equity

Remember News Corp's acquisition of MySpace? That deal had many disastrous aspects, no doubt, but a clue to one of them can be found in MySpace co-founder Tom Anderson's Twitter profile. It reads, "Enjoying being retired." You don't want the Tom Anderson effect to sap your acquisition by giving the founders such a generous payout that they turn off their smartphones and head for the beach.

The solution is to make sure they're paid largely in stock in the enterprise and/or the innovation colony. Payments in stock are usually deferred for a year and vest over several years as an incentive for the team to stay on.

In any case, a portion of the payment is likely to be cash. The purchase price goes first toward paying off the startup's debts, primarily to investors. Whatever is left goes to the startup team. Beyond that, team members generally receive a salary equal to half of what they were getting before.

### Lockups

The team as a whole is more valuable than the sum of its parts, so many contracts include a lockup clause. Under a lockup, teammates don't receive full payment unless they continue to work for a number of years after the deal is signed. Two years is typical. If a single member leaves within that period, the entire team pays the price.

Some founders have no interest in working for an employer and won't remain even through the lockup period. They'll stay only long enough for a press release to be published announcing that their company has been acquired—then they're off like a shot. To avoid this situation, a creative solution might be to stipulate that no press release will be issued until the lockup has passed.

### Earnouts

One of the most controversial acquisition terms is the earnout. This is a set of performance criteria for the startup's business. If they're not met within a specified time, the founders won't receive the full price. An earnout is intended to motivate the founders—a legitimate concern, given that many founders view acquisition as an end game and investors might offer funds to start fresh as soon as the acquisition is consummated. But some acquirers use it to avoid paying them by setting unrealistic benchmarks.

This situation is distressingly common. Disney bought Club Penguin, a virtual world for children, in 2007 for $350 million with an additional $350 million earnout. A year passed without meeting the criteria, and the earnout fell to $175 million. A year after that, Disney ended up with ClubPenguin for $350 million rather than $700 million. Perhaps Disney's expectations were reasonable and ClubPenguin simply failed to execute, but there are times when the abuse is easy to spot. One founder we know agreed to an earnout only to find that the acquirer cut off resources before his company could make its numbers.

This potential for mischief has given earnouts a bad reputation, and founders may view an earnout in your offer as evidence of your untrustworthiness. (On the other hand, they may view it as a way to get a higher number that they can trumpet in the press.) If you insist on an earnout, the best approach is to keep the benchmarks sensible and honor the payment schedule scrupulously.

Incidentally, the longer the founders have been at it, the more sensitive they may be. If they've labored for five years building a startup, they may be loath to surrender it to a new owner. If they've worked on it for a few months and sell it for a king's ransom, they may well figure they can do it again at their leisure.

# Pitfalls

If you've established strong deal flow, selected a solid target, and negotiated a deal that honors both your own company's need for innovation and the startup's accomplishments so far, you're well on your way to a productive acquisition. Nonetheless, there are hidden traps that could keep your deal from leaving the station or derail it before it reaches a payoff. Here are a few to watch out for.

### Losing the CEO

It's hard to overemphasize the importance of keeping the founding CEO onboard. Venture superstar Ben Horowitz writes in his blog about why founding CEOs are the best people to run a startup. "The conventional wisdom says a startup CEO should make way for a professional CEO once the company has achieved product-market fit," he notes. However, at Andreessen Horowitz, "we prefer to fund companies whose founder will run the company as its CEO."

Professional CEOs are skilled at wringing returns out of an innovative business model. Founders may not be so good at maximizing the current opportunity, but they're extraordinarily good at discovering the next one. They have unparalleled knowledge of their companies and their markets, they know how to innovate, and their investment in success is deeply personal. Moreover, they have the tallest bully pulpit: If anyone questions a decision, they have the authority to say, "I created this company. We'll do it my way." This gives them the power to make hard decisions and make them stick.

A Wharton School of Business study concluded that founding CEOs beat professional CEOs on metrics from funding raised to exit valuation. The most successful tech companies bear this out: Adobe, Amazon, Apple, IBM, Facebook, Intel, Microsoft, Oracle, Salesforce, Sony, Twitter, VMWare—all achieved outstanding success under their founding CEOs.

### Moving Too Slowly

As we've seen, speed is everything in the current market. So it's critical to keep the decision-making process around acquisitions streamlined and free of red tape. While you're waiting for board approval, a competitor might swoop in and buy your target, the startup may achieve product/market fit and suddenly have little reason to sell, or an offering that solves the same problem might go viral. In any case, the price could inflate dramatically. GroupMe, a mobile messaging service, raised $850,000 in its first round of debt in August 2010; if that had been equity, it would have given the company a valuation somewhere between $3 million and $5 million. Five months later, the company raised $10.6 million, bringing the valuation to an estimated $50 million—a 10-times increase in five months. When it comes to innovation, there's no upside in waiting.

### Damaging Existing Employee Morale

Paying one engineer $1 million while another makes $100,000 can be toxic to esprit de corps. The atmosphere can become especially poisonous in acqui-hire situations, where the two engineers may end up sitting side by side. If your aim is to encourage existing staff to think big and take risks, give your rank and file a path to making their own millions, making it clear precisely what they need to do to get there. Remember, the ones that are truly interested in that kind of risk/reward profile will seek out opportunities in your innovation colony. Meanwhile, though, you need to keep the staff as a whole happy and productive. The team you're acquiring should be housed in its own space and set to work on its own projects, apart from those of the enterprise at large, to minimize disruptions.

Be sure to structure a deal that aligns incentives of both the startup and the enterprise and take care to avoid these pitfalls. Then your enterprise will have a solid platform for innovation, and your acquisition will be well positioned for hockey-stick growth and immense profits.

---

### Case Study: Neopost, Philippe Boulanger, CTO

As the lean startup movement spreads internationally, enterprises worldwide are beginning to embrace techniques such as rapid experimentation and innovation accounting to innovate more quickly and efficiently. Take Neopost. Founded in 1924 in the United Kingdom and now headquartered in Bagneux, France, the 5,500-person company provides mailroom equipment—postage scales, letter folding machines, postal scanners—to business customers worldwide. CTO Philippe Boulanger manages the transition from analog to digital delivery through a savvy combination of incubation and acquisition. Boulanger used agile development techniques to pioneer a platform approach to Neopost's hardware products, saving costs and reducing development cycles. More recently, he has focused on using lean startup methods to digitize letter and parcel delivery. Below, he explains his approach to acquiring innovative startups.

### *How Would You Describe Your Philosophy of Innovation?*

Everyone can have ideas. What makes a difference is execution. People will tell you, "Oh yes, I had an idea, but somebody else did it." The difference is that somebody did it. What I like about the lean startup machine approach is you innovate by doing things. That is different from just working on a theory and making a business plan that takes ages to unfold. You are experimenting and getting feedback from users.

### *How Is Neopost's Innovation Operation Organized?*

We have 20 R&D sites from Seattle in the United States to Vietnam, which employ something like 800 people. All of them were acquisitions. If you want to keep people, it's important not to say, "We will save a little cost by moving you from Seattle to Connecticut." You are going to lose people by doing that. If you value people and their knowledge, you need to organize yourself so you can keep people where they are and let them continue their work.

### *Do Acquired Companies Keep Their Own Brand Names, or Do They Fall Under the Neopost Brand?*

They keep their brand names and add, "a Neopost company." So they keep their identity, but they become part of the Neopost galaxy. The need to safeguard the brand is a difficulty in big companies. When you do innovation that could be disruptive to the corporation, you are putting the brand image of the company at risk. You are starting something that you might decide to cancel three months later. It can create an image of chaos if you start too many things, present them to customers, then withdraw them from the market soon after. When you are a startup, you have nothing to lose and everything to gain. If you fail, you shut down the company and it is over. If you're in

*(Continued)*

(*Continued*)

a big company and you propose new services to your customers, you are creating a legacy, and you cannot stop. You have a duty to pursue these services for the customers. Most companies I have seen have a hard time stopping activities once they've started. This is most likely slowing down initiatives in big companies.

### Does This Cause a Problem with Shareholders or the CEO, Who May Want the Value Created by Acquisitions to Accrue to the Corporate Brand?

This is not a problem. It is known that these companies are part of the Neopost group.

### What's the Benefit of Acquiring Startups in an Innovation Context?

Acquisition is a way to innovate while managing risk and budget at the same time. When you are making an acquisition, you are purchasing time to market, because people have already done some research and have some products. They have shown some signs of growth or market interest, so you are purchasing credibility as well. All of that has value.

### What Priorities Drive Acquisitions at Neopost?

Considering the potential software and services we could provide to our customers, the span is huge. We cannot work in every direction at the same time. Within the R&D organization, we're working on existing products, maintaining them, and making new revisions. If we are to grow, we need to do more, but the challenge is to find what that more is. We apply lean startup techniques because we know we'll fail multiple times and we'll find something. Alternatively, we can look at what is happening elsewhere and piggyback on that. Usually doing an acquisition means we're taking fewer risks because the target has been already through risky steps in the evolution of their business. And for this reason, we are willing to pay a little bit more.

### The Older a Company Is When You Acquire It, the Less Risk You Take On. The Younger It Is, the More Bang for the Buck You'll Get. How Early Do You Tend to Acquire?

That is a question of tradeoff. Acquiring at the very earliest stage is not necessary for us. Usually, we like to see companies that are already profitable and that will be even more profitable as a result of becoming part of Neopost, or companies that will increase their gross significantly due to working with us.

### Does Your Strategy Differ if You're Looking for Acqui-Hires?

This is not something we have done in the past. By definition, when we make an acquisition, the team is critical. We are very sensitive to make sure the team stays onboard. That team built the startup. It has critical knowledge. We have made some mistakes in the past. We succeeded in killing a few of our first acquisitions, and now we want to make sure they blossom in all possible ways.

### What Were the Mistakes and How Did You Address Them?

We looked too much at synergies based on consolidation instead of synergies that would develop the business. Specifically, we tried to unify the acquisition's sales force with our sales force. We made this mistake at least twice. Also, our earnout plan was too EBIT-driven. The incentive was to continue with the existing product rather than investing in the evolution of the product, which brought the product to an end very quickly. Now earnouts are based not only on EBIT but also on growing the business, the top line as well as the bottom line.

*(Continued)*

(*Continued*)

### How Do You Incentivize the Team to Stay?

Typically through bonuses. The founders have lockup schemes, and they have an earnout if they direct the business in the right way. Usually that works well, from what I have seen.

### How Do You Find Acquisition Opportunities? How Do You Find Acquisition Targets?

Everyone is aware that we're looking, and every opportunity we see is taken into account. We have two processes. First, we identify key strategic directions. We have a number of directions that we already know very well. Once we have decided on that, we scout for companies that are in this direction. Once we have identified a pool of companies in that direction, we dig a bit more to see if one of them is a good fit for us. Some are already way too developed, and we cannot afford them. Some are in the early stage of development, but we have reasons to believe that they will be okay. We get help from marketing and we get help on technical analysis from R&D.

### Do You Have the Power to Approve Acquisitions?

Once we believe we have identified a target, it goes before the staff of the CEO to explain why it is an opportunity and asking to go into due diligence. R&D spending includes R&D intensity, which is a ratio of R&D spending over sales. That is around 4 percent in our industry. I have to stay within this budget whatever I am doing. I have the capacity to choose a little bit inside the budget between the existing business and innovation. From time to time, the opportunity is such that I am allowed to spend more than my committed budget. Every year we have cases where it is worth spending more than what we initially budgeted, and, of course, I request approval for that because the CEO is a financial guy.

My commitment is to have my R&D budget under control, but if an opportunity arises that I cannot fit in my budget, I need to go and explain it.

### Do You Have a Special Approach to Due Diligence?

I think every company has a special way to do it. Basically, we assess risks and opportunities. The basics are financial, looking at every important variable; technical, looking at the processes and technologies being used; and intellectual property: Is it protected, do they have patents, is there a risk of infringing existing patents owned by others?

### Do You Use Innovation Accounting to Evaluate Potential Acquisitions?

The ones we are interested in are already profitable, so they are past the phase where innovation accounting is critical. The conventional accounting scheme works for them.

### How Do You Think About Pricing? Are There Rules of Thumb About What an Acquisition Should Cost?

We are buying companies that are already profitable, so the expectations are realistic. Usually companies are cheaper to acquire in Europe than in the United States. Certainly cheaper than in Silicon Valley. There is still a high premium for high tech, software, and so on, but it's less in Europe.

### What Are the Biggest Pitfalls in Acquiring, and How Do You Avoid Them?

Your initial expectations about a company are based on the first meetings. Then you have to make up your mind about the reality. If the founders want to sell the company, they present

*(Continued)*

*(Continued)*

it in a nice way. In France, we would say the bride is beautiful. The bride may be too beautiful to be true if she has a lot of makeup. So the biggest risk is not going into enough depth in the due diligence process to discover the truth about the bride. We have done due diligence on companies that we didn't acquire in the end. What we learned was not in line with our initial expectations, and this was already a bad sign. I think we are doing well. All of our acquisitions in the past two years have had double-digit growth.

# Chapter 11

# Invest When You Can't Acquire

So you've identified a startup that's aligned with your enterprise's innovation thesis, and it has all the requisite elements to make an impact: a solid team with outstanding vision, excellent technical capabilities, a flair for execution, and a product that has been developed to the brink of fitting hand-in-glove with paying customers.

Just one hitch.' *The damn founders don't want to sell.* Maybe they're confident that they're just about to break through to a receptive market, and the investment community is piling on. Maybe they've put so much of themselves personally into their startup that they can't imagine fitting into a foreign corporate structure. Maybe they don't trust a big company with their baby.

Or maybe you don't want to buy. You see immense potential value, but it's too early. The product is underdeveloped or the target market

185

is fiercely contested. You want to share in its prospects, but you're not ready to purchase outright.

At this point, the third enterprise innovation strategy comes into play: Invest when you can't acquire. Face it, the next Facebook is not going to let an enterprise buy it wholesale. But it may be happy to take your money, and the investment can bring significant advantages in terms of both return and partnership down the line. Meanwhile, a creative, aggressive startup that hasn't yet found its feet can make good use of the funding and surrender a bigger slice of the pie. And you'll be in a perfect position to monitor its progress and evaluate whether it's consistently driving key metrics in the right direction, and to make a persuasive acquisition offer when the time is right.

## Low Control, High Momentum

As we saw in Strategy (Chapter 2), investment offers the lowest degree of control. As an investor, you'll likely own well under 49 percent of the startup. You may be awarded a seat on the board of directors, but even in that case, your influence over the startup's direction will be limited. And your potential upside will be correspondingly limited.

On the other hand, investment offers maximum momentum. Compared with incubating internally and acquiring, it's less expensive and your investment is substantially de-risked. After all, the team, its capabilities, and its track record are already established. You have ample evidence on which to base your decisions. And you have the opportunity to climb aboard a rocket—and pour additional fuel into the tank— just as it's blasting off. It may yet blow up, but all systems are "go."

Rakutan, Japan's largest online retailer, made that kind of bet on Pinterest in May 2012, when it led a $100 million Series C round that included Andreessen Horowitz, Bessemer Venture Partners, and FirstMark Capital. Pinterest is the kind of dark-horse challenger that could severely damage online retailers. Unlike an online store, it nudges users toward purchasing as they browse during spare moments. Moreover, Rakutan CEO Hiroshi Mikitani says, Pinterest, through its sheer entertainment value, has the power to reactivate disengaged customers and revital-ize moribund product categories, and it promises to become a powerful conduit for mobile commerce. Since Rakutan's investment, Pinterest's valuation had more than doubled from $1.5 billion to $3.8 billion as of late 2013—an already healthy appreciation that's likely to balloon with Pinterest's seemingly inevitable IPO.

## Benefits of Investing

Investing in what you can't or aren't ready to acquire is the easiest of the three and probably the one to set your sights on first. On the other hand, of the three enterprise innovation strategies, it offers the least upside potential. It gives the enterprise less say in important decisions, such as when to persevere or pivot, which could have a material impact on its business.

But even this low-control strategy can realize an outsized return on investment. That's what Microsoft did when, in 2007, it bought 1.6 percent of a college-dorm startup called Facebook for $240 million. At the time, the world of social networking indisputably belonged to MySpace, a property of Rupert Murdoch's News Corp. Viacom had stepped out on a limb to offer $1.5 billion for 100 percent of Facebook less than two years earlier, so the valuation in light of Microsoft's investment, which amounted to 10 times that amount, seemed outrageous. Today it's clear that Microsoft got a steal: Facebook's market cap was $155 billion as of January 2014, making Redmond's stake worth $2.48 billion. What's more, the relationship led to Facebook embracing Microsoft's Bing search engine rather than Google's. Not bad for an investment widely considered ridiculously overpriced!

## Investment Mechanics

Investing is certainly the quickest way to act on your innovation thesis. Entrepreneurs are frequently on the hunt for capital, and you can pitch into most startups at any time.

How much should you invest? A number between $50,000 and $300,000 is typical for early-stage backing. The median angel round in the second quarter of 2013 was $590,000, according to the Angel Capital Association.

As for what kind of return you can expect, plan for the best. No doubt, this advice sounds counterintuitive. But if you invest in a company that goes bankrupt, your loss is limited to the money you put up. If you fail to invest in the next Apple or Google, the lack of return could amount to billions.

Consider Peter Thiel. In 2004, he put $500,000 to Facebook's initial round, buying 10 percent of the company. However, he stayed out of the next round. That initial investment was worth nearly $15.5 billion as of January 2014, but his stake could have been worth many times more if he had contributed to the next round. The lost opportunity must have hurt: Thiel has invested in every Facebook equity round since.

## Investment Vehicles

There are two ways to invest. You can extend a loan that later will be restructured as equity (known as a convertible note), or you can purchase equity outright. Each approach has benefits and drawbacks.

### Convertible Notes

An early-stage startup is difficult to price. At the very beginning, it has little to no value—its value is all potential. If you're buying a slice of a company that has no substantial assets or revenue, how can you calculate the size of the piece your money buys? A convertible note solves this problem. Convertible notes are still uncommon in enterprise investing, but they've become a standard practice among very early-stage investors.

The utility of a convertible note isn't limited to the period before the company has an established value. It also lets you invest between equity rounds, when the startup's value may be in flux. Say, the company needs cash to tide it over between Series A and Series B, but it's growing so fast that the Series A valuation is already clearly too low. A convertible note enables you to get in before the next round.

Here's how it works: You give the startup a quantity of cash, say, $100,000, without specifying the portion of the company that it represents. The startup puts the investment to use to facilitate growth, and presumably its value increases. As the company grows and amasses assets and revenue, it builds a rational basis for determining its value. This attracts other investors who put up, say, $1 million for a 10 percent stake. This implies that the company is worth $10 million, and your initial loan converts into a 1 percent share of equity.

That said, there is a hitch. What if the new investors put up $10 million for 10 percent? In this case, your stake would only be worth one-tenth of 1 percent. To protect yourself against the risk that your stake might be diluted in this way, you'll want to set a cap on the valuation at the time you make your investment. For instance, if you're investing in a company that already has an established value, and the last round settled on a $1 million valuation and the next round seems likely to bring it to $10 million, you might negotiate a $5 million cap.

Now comes the good part. Fueled by the cash infusion, the company is able to iterate on its product development effort more rapidly and efficiently. Before long, it achieves product/market fit, and it takes off. Assets and revenue grow by leaps and bounds. Another round of investors put up $100 million for a 10 percent stake, and the value of your 1 percent expands from $100,000 to $1 million.

The startup might not prosper. The next rounds of investors may not show up, and the founders may decide to pack it in. What happens then? If they find a buyer, creditors will be first in line to take some of the purchase price, so you're likely to get some or all of your money back. If not, you're out of luck. You'll write off the investment as a loss.

The primary benefit of investing via convertible note is speed. Unlike an equity round, a convertible note can be cut at any time. It's a one-on-one transaction, so it's far simpler to execute. There are fewer legal documents to be negotiated, vetted, and signed, and the money can be deposited in the startup's account immediately. It's also lower-risk, since debts are paid off before preferred stock if the startup ultimately liquidates.

On the other hand, follow-on rounds can dilute your investment, so you need to set the cap carefully. (Founders may see risk in the investor's conflict of interest: As an investor, you want to do everything in your power to help the startup grow; but your investment's value shrinks as the startup's value grows, so you also have an incentive to stymie that growth. This isn't likely to be a problem assuming that your ethical compass is true, but you should know that it may weigh on the founders' minds.)

## Equity Investments

In an equity deal, you pay a particular sum for a specific percentage of the company. Generally, startups raise equity in rounds, and the deal isn't done until the round is complete, which may involve lining up several investors. A startup may take its time looking for name-brand investors to lead or join a round, and a fast-growing venture has an incentive to delay the round as its potential value climbs, which can slow things down further. Thus, you can't buy equity on your own schedule. The startup and its other funders control the timing.

The main advantage of equity investing is that, unlike investment via convertible note, the startup has a tangible market value. Your stake is based on that, so you know how much of the company you're buying. Another advantage is that your check is just one of several. The company receives far more capital than you're putting up, and the additional runway serves to reduce your risk. Also, as a shareholder, you have a right to receive regular financial statements and to audit the company's books, and possibly a seat on the board of directors, which can substantially increase your involvement and potential influence over the startup's direction.

It's worth noting that participants in initial equity rounds often receive a right of first refusal in follow-on rounds. Early-stage rounds tend to involve small amounts of money, and joining them can be an inexpensive way to get in line for a more substantial stake down the line. In fact, VCs often invest early just to gain the option to participate in the next funding round. You can choose not to double down if the price is too high, but you've locked in the opportunity, and that may open the door to a very lucrative investment.

These advantages weigh against the fact that you can't invest until the startup initiates a fundraising round. Also, in the event of a liquidation, you won't be entitled to your money until the startup's debts have been paid.

## Enterprise Investment Psychology

One thing to know before forging ahead into an early-stage investment is that startup founders in general don't trust corporate investors. Enterprises, unlike well-connected, highly experienced venture investors, are perceived to add little or no value beyond the money they offer. Fred Wilson, cofounder of Union Square Ventures, advises founders that dealing with corporate venture funds is a waste of time. The managing directors of Techstars (a Lean Startup Machine investor) caution entrepreneurs that corporate investors can steal their ideas or block them from getting additional capital down the line. Mark Suster of Upfront Ventures (also an investor in Lean Startup Machine) calls the phrase *strategic investor* an oxymoron. This puts you at a disadvantage in any investment negotiation.

Why all the hate? The reasons are straightforward. In general, corporate investors don't add value beyond the capital they provide. Angels, seed-stage funding organizations, and VCs, on the other hand, bring expertise and networks of potential mentors, services, and partners as well as the possibility of further funding. Moreover, corporate investors, unlike typical angels or venture fund partners, have no skin in the game personally and serve at the pleasure of their organization. They might be here today and gone tomorrow, so they aren't well positioned to serve as a resource to the companies they invest in. And corporate politics can play havoc with the companies they invest in.

Mark Suster describes a typical horror story in a blog post:

> One month after investing, the guy who invested left his firm. The guy who took over said, "I never believed we should invest in dot-coms. I will be on your board but don't ask me for anything." His words were an understatement. He fought me for three years and actively worked against our interests. I struggled to get every signature or consent. The market knew he was an investor yet he wouldn't promote us within his own company. You can imagine how that made us look in the German market, where his company is a big deal.

The upshot is twofold. First, as a strategic investor, you should be ready to offer generous terms. Ambitious founders may feel that they can look elsewhere, so you need to make the deal worth their while.

Second, you can't afford to weigh a startup's valuation too heavily in your decisions. Nor should you, given the upside potential. Many investors try to mitigate their risk by driving for a low price or advantageous terms such as a liquidation preferences. But such advantages don't amount to much in the face of a 10,000x return. Remember the power law: One blockbuster will more than make up for the lesser startups in your portfolio. Y Combinator didn't pick its top performers, but it did invest early. If you lose, you lose 1x. If you win, you gain 10,000x. It's that simple. You're buying into the potential for rapid, exponential growth, and that's what you should optimize for.

# Choosing Investments

With 225,000 active angels and 460-plus venture capital (VC) firms operating in the United States, you might think the field of start-ups has been picked clean by other investors. It hasn't. The opportunities are plentiful and bursting with potential. That's because many early-stage investors use imprecise criteria in choosing where to put their money.

At Lean Startup Machine, we asked more than 50 investors how they vet potential investments. Very few said they built financial models or spoke with customers. Instead, they said they look at the team with an eye toward whether it had the skills and determination to build a profitable business.

This may have made sense in the past, when proven techniques for growing startups had yet to be developed. Skilled leadership is still necessary, but it's not the only thing or even the most important thing. The lean startup method provides a roadmap to product/market fit that transcends the team executing it.

## *Evaluating Product/Market Fit*

The key is to evaluate targets using research (see Experimental Methods (Chapter 7)) and metrics modeling (see Innovation Accounting (Chapter 8)). In an investment scenario, the research method is likely to be customer interviews. In a nutshell, this means finding customers, asking them questions, and probing their problems and how well the product solves them. The idea behind metrics modeling is to simulate the business according to the principles of innovation accounting.

Start by building a spreadsheet model that describes how user behaviors generate revenue. Then enter fictional metrics that represent an ideal case. Then gather real-world numbers from the founders and enter those. By comparing the real and ideal cases, you can see how well the actual business matches the ideal and thus how close it is to product/market fit.

When the real and ideal cases match, the startup no longer needs to figure out what to build or how to scale the business. It's no longer dealing with extreme uncertainty. It may not have the best product in the world, but the product it has is substantially de-risked.

### Make Your Own Decisions

The investors we surveyed also said they looked for social proof. That is, if other investors put their money into a particular startup, that venture must be a good bet. This is an archaic way to go about evaluating investments in the information age. Worse, it's a barrier to learning. You'll never learn how to choose investments wisely if you don't study them in light of your innovation thesis, test your hypotheses, and make your own decisions based on what you find. Make your investments carefully and methodically, study your successes and failures, and apply the lessons learned when making your next investment.

In fact, investor reliance on social proof can hurt entrepreneurs when word gets out that they've been passed up. Keep this in mind when you approach founders to discuss making an investment. Let them know you'll be making your own decision, that you don't care about what other investors think and won't be approaching them to ask their opinions. This will minimize their worry that, if you evaluate their company and then decide not to make a deal, your decision will put off other potential benefactors.

These techniques aren't rocket science, but they can be like rocket fuel for your investment strategy. The secret is not in the team's chemistry or what other investors think; it's in the interaction between the product and its market. Plenty of startups have great teams and marquee investors, yet they go nowhere. But few businesses whose metrics add up to clear market value are likely to fail.

## Case Study: Intel Capital, Marlon Nichols, Kauffman Fellow

Intel Capital is an innovation juggernaut by any reckoning. With $850 million in assets under management, the venture arm of Intel Corporation has been the second most active corporate VC since 2009, according to CB Insights, with investments spanning hardware and software in the consumer Internet, cloud, data center, digital media, manufacturing, mobile, open source, security, and wearable markets. In 2011, the organization established a $300 million fund to promote the ecosystem around ultrabooks—thin, lightweight, power-efficient, touch-screen-equipped laptop computers—and in 2013 allocated a $100 million fund to experiences and perceptual computing, fostering applications that sense touch, gesture, voice, and emotion. Marlon Nichols is charged with leading seed-stage activities for these funds. The opinions he expresses are his own and not those of Intel.

### How Does Intel's Investment Strategy Fit in with the Broader Innovation Effort?

The way we go about investments is twofold. First, we're always looking for companies we believe will be market leaders, strong revenue generators. At the same time, we're looking for companies that are relevant to Intel in some way. I give this a lot of latitude, because Intel is involved in so many different businesses and has a history of moving in, and sometimes out, of new areas. Is this company producing a product that Intel can leverage? Is it part of an ecosystem that needs to be developed before Intel can dive in? Is it useful in helping us think about the future?

### Are Investments Coordinated with Acquisition and Incubation Efforts?

Intel is acquisitive, but when we go into an investment, we're not interested in buying the company in a couple of years. If that's the mind-set from day one, we'd lead with an acquisition rather than an equity deal. So we look for ways—hopefully we identify them early in the relationship—that Intel Corp might be interested in working with the portfolio company.

### What's Your Investment Thesis?

There are a number of them throughout Intel Capital. We have investment groups focused on mobile, security, data centers, and so on, and each one aligns to a corresponding business unit of Intel Corp. The investment thesis for each of those organizations is different. We do have the concept of eyes and ears; we're making investments that educate the business units on what tomorrow might look like. In my sector, Ultrabooks and Perceptual Computing, we're looking for companies that are creating new experiences on ultrabooks, two-in-ones, and other devices. There's a big emphasis on the concept of context, devices leveraging what's going on around you to become smarter, and presenting you with options that make sense for your current situation. We're also interested in 3D imaging, emotion sensing, biometrics, immersive collaboration, and other next-generation capabilities.

### How Did You Formulate That Thesis?

It comes from Intel's understanding that the user experience is very important in this world of mobility. What makes the difference between buying one device or another, or this software or that software, is the experience it delivers. It's a much more end-user centric marketplace these days, in my opinion.

### What Are You Looking for in Early-Stage Investments?

It's the same for making later-stage investments. The main thing is a market. Is this company addressing a net-new problem, creating a market, and can that market be a large one? Also, if it's not net-new, is it around disrupting something that's already

*(Continued)*

(*Continued*)

a large market? Will consumers gravitate to it? Will they buy it? Can it be a $500 million to $1 billion company? Those figures would amount to a good investment for a venture fund. At the end of the day, you need to provide significant return to the fund. You're trying to create value for your stakeholders. If you're in an institutional fund, that means your limited partners; in a corporate venture firm, it's your sole limited partner. Then the next thing is the team. Is this a group of smart people? Can they make the necessary adjustments? Do they know the space they're trying to get into better than most? Then it's competition and differentiation. What are they doing that's unique? Is it easily replicated? If not, how protected is it? If it's not defensible, how much of a runway can they establish? And will that be meaningful enough for them to sustain advantage in the market? Those are the three things you look for initially.

### Strategic Investors Have a Bad Rap in the Startup Community. What's the Key to Being a Good Strategic Investor?

Don't impose entrepreneur-unfriendly terms. Follow through on promises. Make relevant and impactful introductions. Regularly attend and contribute at the board level. Be generally available and supportive to portfolio companies. Recognize that you are in a partnership with company and the other investors—treat it as such.

### How Do You Convince Your Targets That You're a Worthy Investor?

I can't speak for all strategic investors, only for Intel Capital. We think about investments in terms of the long haul. We made 52 new investments and 72 follow-on investments in 2013. So we made 20 more follow-on investments in our current portfolio than we made new investments. That suggests that we take care of our companies and support them along the way. We add value in other ways, as well. First and foremost, we're connected to Intel Corp, which has broad reach in terms of relationships. A portfolio company would be hard-pressed to find a technology company they wanted to be connected to that we don't have a relationship with. We hold Intel Capital Technology Days where we bring in a customer such as Microsoft, BMW, or Warner Bros, that's looking for early-stage companies to partner with to solve a challenge, and we invite portfolio companies that have solutions relevant to that challenge. At the end of the meeting, the customer companies can decide which portfolio companies they want to follow up with. The majority of the portfolio companies walk away with a second meeting, and a good percentage of those end up working with that customer company. Being able to sit in a room with a CIO of a Global 200 is a big deal for a tech startup. We also hold an annual Intel Capital Global Summit, where we invite executives from both portfolio companies and other global organizations to spend a week together. More than 2,300 meetings took place at our 2013 event.

### What Benefits Does Intel Corp Get from Strategic Investments?

There's a financial return associated with our investments—it can be additional revenue coming into the company. Also, we are the company's eyes and ears, providing opportunities to see new technology long before it's written up in major periodicals. Additionally, Intel may be working on a particular technology and, by the way, a portfolio company has developed an innovative solution that can drive a better result for our customers. There's also the concept of ecosystem development. Intel can create a chipset that supports 3D imaging, but if there isn't an accompanying, compelling experience, it is unlikely that consumers will reach into their wallets. So, it's prudent to invest in companies that can help to drive those experiences.

### How Often Do You Take a Seat on the Board of a Company You've Invested In?

It depends on whether we led the deal and the size of our participation. We prefer to lead, and if we do, it makes sense

*(Continued)*

*(Continued)*

to take a board seat. If we're joining a syndicate as a minority investor, we may opt not to. Whether we take a board seat or board observer seat, we aim to drive as much value as possible. That's evident in the fact that we had something like 26 exits in 2013; 22 of those were M&A transactions, and the other four were IPOs. You don't get there unless you're helping the companies to build and grow.

### What Benefits Come with a Board Seat?

I don't know that it's necessarily better being on the board or observing. In both cases, you're privy to a lot of information regarding the direction, health, and performance of the company, and you're suggesting to the management team what can be done to help. The big difference is that a board member has a vote and an observer doesn't. But an effective board observer can still influence a vote. Bottom line is always to do what's best for the company.

### How Do You Build Deal Flow?

The best source of deal flow is entrepreneurs. CEOs and founders you've worked with in the past can introduce you to folks who are starting companies, or entrepreneurs you're working with can introduce you to other entrepreneurs. I do a lot of work with accelerators, coaching and mentoring their companies to make connections with the entrepreneurs. Some will go on to be successful, and they'll remember the time you spent with them. Other venture firms and partners can be good deal sources as well.

### How Long Does It Take, on Average, Between Learning About a Potential Investment and Completing the Transaction?

I've seen deals get done in two weeks, but you want to avoid rushing through diligence unless you absolutely have to. Always remember that you're optimizing for the long term, so it's important to truly understand the business and the people you're investing in. A seed-stage deal takes roughly four weeks. A typical time frame for a series A or B deal is six weeks, but it depends on the complexity of the deal among other things.

### Under What Circumstances Would You Invest via Convertible Note, and Under What Circumstances Would You Do a Straight Equity Deal?

Most seed-stage deals use a convertible note vehicle. For Series A and beyond, most deals are priced. It depends on the phase the company is in at the time of the investment.

### What Is the Typical Size of a Strategic Investment?

There's no typical size. Most seed-stage companies raise between $250,000 and $2.5 million. Series A or B, maybe between $5 million and $10 million. But it depends on a lot of variables: how fast the company is growing, what its potential is, the market's appetite for the company at a particular valuation, how much it needs to raise to be successful, software versus hardware.

### What's the Highest Return You've Received So Far? What Multiple Did You Achieve?

Intel Capital has seen many positive returns with 534 exits in 20-plus years. Some of those companies include VMWare, Red Hat, MySQL, and Citrix. The cycle is roughly five to eight years, and I've only been here for three, but hopefully I'll have the opportunity to realize similar success.

# Chapter 12

# Innovation Flow

I n the preceding chapters we covered philosophical, structural, and procedural aspects of running lean enterprise innovation colonies. But generating sufficient innovation flow to generate hits is a challenge. You need access to a steady stream of ideas that harmonize well with prevailing business currents. Insight into those currents is provided by the innovation colony's network of angels, accelerators, VCs, and entrepreneurs, as well as the colonists' own expertise and insights. If only one in 1,000 ideas has a chance to succeed, then you need to choose your targets from among thousands of prospects. That's a high number, but it's not out of reach. Even a small colony can get there, and a large one can sift through correspondingly larger numbers of ideas.

The initial size of an innovation colony depends on the enterprise's means and priorities. Most companies will be able to fund only a modest undertaking, while others will be ready to form a full-scale operation right off the bat. We think it makes sense to start small and grow as the colony begins producing successful results.

But no matter what size you start at, generating that flow of ideas will be a challenge. You'll need to consider thousands of solid opportunities before you find one that explodes. Here's a plan for developing that capacity. The ideas themselves can come from suggestion boxes, brainstorming sessions, hackathons, and Lean Startup Machine events as detailed in Incubate Internally (Chapter 9), or through close interactions with the investment and startup communities, as described in Acquire Early (Chapter 10) and Invest When You Can't Acquire (Chapter 11). In any case, you'll need a colony that's right-sized to manage whatever innovation flow can generate.

For those who want to start with an innovation Nauru (the world's smallest island nation) and work their way up to a United Federation of Planets, we propose building out in four stages, from a minimally funded trial to an extravagantly capitalized innovation factory (Visit http://theleanenterprisebook.com/resources for more information.). The budget at each stage forms a finite runway designed to spur urgency and encourage thrift. The aim is to build innovation flow based on large numbers of modest expenditures. Strict limitations on available funding encourage early moves to acquire or invest and a disciplined attitude toward evaluating the prospect of product/market fit regardless of how a startup originates.

The four stages place graduated constraints on incubator staff size, number of acquisitions, and number of investments. Stage 1 is a $5-million, two-year trial. The next three stages ramp up to $20 million over five years, $50 million over five years, and $100 million over a decade respectively. At each stage, the budget apportions 40 percent to incubation, 20 percent to acquisition, and 40 percent to investment. These percentages are guidelines, not rules, and you can feel free to adjust them according to your needs. (Note that one long-term aim is to develop a competency for incubation, and the other two strategies are largely means to that end, shedding light on market trends and opening doors to talent and partnerships.)

For our purpose, a startup is defined as an investment, an acquisition, or an internal project that has been incubated to the point of setting baseline metrics.

Stage 1: The first stage is a limited-cost proof of concept. Its purpose is to test the managing directors and the organization in progress. Spending $5 million over two years, you can allocate $2 million each to investments and incubation and $1 million to acquisitions. Investing between $25,000 and $50,000 at a time, you can select some 60 investments from a pool of, say, 10- to 20-times that number of opportunities. The incubation budget allows for five teams of two to three people each, assuming an average salary of $75,000. If they pivot every two months (that is, if it takes them that long on average to reach the point of setting baseline metrics), they can evaluate 64 startups over two years. With a $1 million acquisition budget, they can acqui-hire one or two teams priced between $500,000 and $1 million each, selected from 5- to 10-times that number of startups. That gives you roughly 120 shots selected from approximately 1,200 possibilities.

Because the two-year time horizon is relatively short, the success criterion is to secure follow-on funding for 50 percent to 70 percent of startups per year. (Seventy percent of Techstars companies receive follow-on funding.) If all goes well, after two years, the directors will get an additional $15 million and move on to Stage 2.

Stage 2: The second stage is a $20 million vote of confidence in the nascent innovation colony. The investment allocation is $8 million over five years, enough for 240 bets. With eight teams, the incubator can test roughly 256 startups selected, again, from 10- to 20-times that number of prospects. In addition, we can acquire between four and eight companies or teams chosen from 5- to 10-times that number. In this stage, the colony tests nearly 500 startups from as many as 5,000 options. In Stages 2, 3, and 4, the goal is to generate 19 percent growth per year, on average, matching the average top quartile of venture capital (VC) earnings from 2007-2011, according to Cambridge Associates. That validates the colony's effectiveness and leads to Stage 3.

Stage 3: Continuing on to the $50-million funding level, the innovation colony is investing $20 million in some 480 independent startups. A 53-person staff—forming 21 teams—invests $20 million to test 640 original startups and spends $10 million on between 10 and 20 acquisitions. At the end of five years, the colony will have launched more than 1,120 projects from as many as 11,200 possibilities. A few hits, not to mention a plethora of minor successes, would bring a healthy return on investment.

Stage 4: This is a full-scale, $100-million innovation continent scheduled to rise like Atlantis over 10 years. The investment effort buys stakes in roughly 9,600 companies maximizing the chance of catching a few rising stars. The bulk of investing is likely to take place within the first three to five years, giving them time to pay off within the 10-year term. The incubation staff now numbers 106, divided into 42 or so teams and capable of fostering 1,280 startups. The acquisition budget covers up to 40 acqui-hired teams, although you may conceivably spend as much as $10 million or $20 million for hot properties whose products you want to bring into the fold. Startups in the colony's control now total 2,280 chosen from roughly 10 times that number.

This seems to us to be a practical ceiling on innovation colony size given the organizational structure we've outlined (see Corporate Structure (Chapter 3)), but we don't have any real evidence to back that up. The largest VC funds have consistently outperformed their smaller rivals over the past decade. Perhaps bigger will prove better in innovation colonies as well.

Corporations that reach Stage 4 and beyond will be ready to innovate on a grand scale, with all strategies in play and lean startup principles guiding development on all fronts. They will take advantage of state-of-the-art techniques to stay on top of technological change, develop highly desirable products, and bring them to large numbers of customers at the lowest possible cost. They will pioneer a new era in which the innovative capacity of society at large will be utilized more efficiently than ever before and large companies will routinely out-innovate smaller rivals. This is the ultimate promise of the lean enterprise.

---

### Case Study: Intuit, Bennett Blank, Innovation Leader

Bennett Blank joined Intuit as an interaction designer in 2007, and since then he has helped build the company's innovation infrastructure from a small team focused on a single department into a network of programs for fostering new products from the bottom up. Intuit's unique emphasis on grassroots innovation allows it to generate high numbers of fresh ideas outside the structure of business as usual, resulting in tens of millions of dollars in additional revenue (by the company's reckoning) with the promise of much, much more to come. Blank is a driving force in scaling up that capacity. He views it as his job to "take the innovation mojo and spread it across the company," and he took time out to tell us how he does it.

### What's Your Personal Approach to Innovation?

Most innovative ideas come from a unique insight about the customer. I start by taking time to understand a customer's hopes, fears, and dreams beyond the task they're trying to complete. That gives you a foundation for exploring a wide variety of potential opportunities. Then you can formulate a series of specific problem statements that you can test with the customer to see if you're improving the world in some way. It's about starting with something high level, big, and bold, something that's worth your time and effort, and moving forward as quickly as you can to test whether or not the solution you have in mind will be valuable.

### How Does Intuit Deal with the Typical Corporate Barriers to Innovation?

Intuit faces the same challenges as any large organization. We attack them by creating a grassroots culture. Everyone is allowed to spend 10 percent of their time on anything that they're passionate about, so everyone is empowered to come up with ideas and at least get started developing them. We train everyone in the company to develop their ideas through a program called Design for Delight, which is our internal version of design thinking. The program focuses on three principles: customer empathy, exploring lots of opportunities, and rapid experimentation with customers. Employees who need help can call on coaches, and we have outlets for unstructured time, events that last from two days to a week, where people can

*(Continued)*

(*Continued*)

work on projects with mentorship from other engineers and designers. We run into challenges deciding which ideas to fund or how to balance new ideas with existing priorities. That will always be a challenge. But Intuit gives employees space to get started as well as guidelines for moving forward. You can't necessarily launch a brand new product and start collecting revenue on your own, but you can certainly form a team, talk to customers, and run experiments.

### *Where Do Ideas Come From? How Do You Generate Them?*

Ideas come from everywhere, period, end of the story. Whether the janitor or the CEO, everyone has equal opportunity to explore an idea. Sometimes we'll do a challenge. A business leader will say, "I want to re-imagine QuickBooks"—I'm making that up—or, "I'm looking for ideas around x." We might hold an Idea Jam, which is a brainstorming session focused on a particular issue. We're inspired by the problems and issues our customers are dealing with, but it also by research. We try our best to look outside as well as inside. "Follow me home" is a phrase we use to describe any process where we go outside of Intuit and watch customers in the wild. It's been in our DNA for 30 years, and everybody understands it as part of our culture. It doesn't mean that we go to customers' houses, but we go out into the world and watch customers dealing with challenges in their daily life. If you do one of those sessions, you may come away with four or five new ideas.

### *How Do Employees Form Teams?*

We have an internal tool called Brainstorm, a social network for ideas that connects employees so they can collaborate. If I'm really busy and don't have time for innovation, I don't need to log in. But if I have a break in my schedule, I can look for something to use my unstructured time on, or if I have an inspiration for a product that I think customers will love, I can enter it and find other people who might be interested in helping. It connects people based on the project they're working on. If it's an iPhone app, I can search for people who are also interested in building iPhone apps. I can say, "Trevor, I see you're interested in iPhone apps and you work in the payments group. My idea is related to mobile payments. What do you think?" Then we can discuss it. Trevor might say, "We've already tried that and it didn't work," or "Your idea is similar to this project that's already going on," and I can join the team. As the person running an idea, I can share it and invite people to contribute or join my team.

### How Does an Idea Become Commercialized?

The ideas people are working on cover the entire spectrum from incremental, sustaining innovations to big, bold, new-to-the-world ideas. Sustaining innovations often get absorbed by the team members' business unit, and often they're implemented. We have many stories of small ideas that save a couple of million dollars here and there or give us a bump in conversion. For big, bold ideas, the teams try to gather as much evidence as they can that this is an idea Intuit should consider. At some point, they'll engage a business lead or product manager, someone they think would be a good outlet for the product. "We think we have something here. We've run a couple of experiments and it's going well. What do you guys think?" I wouldn't say it's casual, but it's not a formal CEO-and-board review.

### What Criteria Are Used Determine Whether to Invest Substantial Funds?

The hope is that through this process, the ideas that are most valuable will be self-evident. Most ideas aren't particularly

*(Continued)*

(*Continued*)

good, and that's okay. The teams will self-select and say, "Our idea isn't so good," while another team will say, "Ours has some traction." If it's in their own space, they can implement it, and then they have to put it in a presentation or put it on someone's roadmap. Otherwise, they have to present evidence that gives the executives confidence that it's worth pursuing.

### *What About Ideas That Are Highly Disruptive?*

If an idea is too far afield, it can be tough for folks to see how we can get there or why it's important to us. That's a challenge. Ideally, the team would generate enough evidence to show that this makes sense for Intuit, that there's some durable competitive advantage in it. If it's outside our space and doesn't align with our mission to improve the financial lives of customers, it probably wouldn't get funded—not because it's a bad idea, but because we need to serve our mission.

### *Assuming That It's Better to Have More Ideas Than Fewer, How Do You Scale Up to Process Greater Numbers of Ideas?*

We're trying to let the processing take place with the people who generate the ideas. The chance that we can pick winners is as low as the chance that anyone else can, so why would we do that? The teams find out quickly that an idea isn't good, the market isn't ready, the customer isn't who they expected, the implementation isn't quite right, or whatever. There are tons of ideas in Brainstorm that teams have explored and decided not to pursue. It's not like we say, "We've found your idea, please come pitch to us." It's more like, "Here's an opportunity if you're interested." The team has to lead the way.

### *What Success Stories Can You Tell Us?*

There's a product called SparkRent. A couple of folks had the idea, gosh, paying rent ought to be easier. They captured their idea in Brainstorm and attended a Lean StartIN, a two-day event where they developed the idea through rapid experimentation with customers. They ran a few simple experiments and learned that there was interest from landlords and tenants. They continued to pursue the idea and built enough evidence that they convinced their business unit to give them a little more time, beyond 10 percent, to work on it. They carved out more and more space, to the point that now it's a live product that's generating revenue. The important part of the story is that it started with a few folks who used these innovation principles to make consistent progress on their own until they got more resources. Over about 18 months, they built a case that Intuit should keep it going. In other organizations, you pick a winner, pitch the winner, get $10 million, and execute. That's not how we do it. You ask for a dollar, you spend it. Then you ask for three and spend that. Then you ask for five. You build your case over time rather than going for the big win.

### What's the Next Step in the Evolution of Your Innovative Process?

Lots of things came together to ignite our innovation spark. The cultural foundation was set, then the lean startup method came along. Now the grassroots effort has really picked up steam. The next phase is about focusing it on big opportunities. Of the products that are starting to get to market, we have yet to identify the next QuickBooks or TurboTax. Now that ideas are bubbling up, we need to double down on the ones that gain traction and give teams even more opportunities to pursue them on their own. We're unlocking the ability to get to the next level.

### What Will Intuit Look Like When the System Is Running at Full Tilt?

Scott Cook, Intuit's founder, wants to leave behind a company that generates new ideas from the bottom up, because

*(Continued)*

(*Continued*)

that's more sustainable than running from the top down. It's a longer view. You've got to invest in the whole company. But, over time, we believe it's a better strategy. It's leaning into what Intuit is best at. We have multiple business units, we're a matrix organization, all those structural things. Instead of trying to change that, we're trying to judo it into an innovation process that works for us.

# Conclusion

The notion of creating an independent entity to manage, execute, and profit from innovation with little direction from the enterprise or cooperation with existing business units challenges some of the most deeply held values of corporate culture. It's difficult to accept that a successful, long-standing, highly respected, and deeply experienced organization has nothing beyond financing to offer its fledgling innovation division.

Over the course of discussing the ideas in this book with enterprise executives, we encountered enthusiastic support, but also objections, many of which influenced our approach to the innovation colony concept and the lean startup process itself. We've listened to executives bemoan the lack of entrepreneurial spirit among employees and their employees carp over lack of support for internal entrepreneurship, and we've concluded that a separate innovative entity is the best approach. We've watched enterprises throw all their energy into making incremental gains while smaller, leaner organizations redefined their industry. We respect the power of a great brand, stellar distribution, and financial firepower, but they're largely impotent in the absence of groundbreaking business ideas that have been developed to product/market fit. At that point, however, an enterprise's strengths can be brought to bear in a way that few startups will be able to match.

In the next several pages, we examine some of the most common objections and explain why the enterprise has much to gain by pursuing innovation according to the principles and methods we describe. We also look at some deeper implications. When enterprises consistently create radically new products, open new markets, and spark new industries, they have a sweeping impact on the innovation ecosystem.

## Objections to the Lean Enterprise

Arguments against the lean enterprise are largely driven by a failure to appreciate the profound changes in the worlds of product development and marketing in recent decades. Let's consider the most common objections in turn.

### Objection: Existing Organization Can Handle Innovation

Enterprise executives have a hard time accepting the need to build a separate structure for innovation. They run a successful operation and they don't understand why that's not enough. They're proud of their company, and rightly so. And they like to be in control—after all, that's what they're good at.

The problem is that the enterprise environment is geared for execution. But innovation is a process of discovery that must take place *before* execution can come into play. Study after study shows that corporations can't disrupt their own business from within. The resources and practices that are the lifeblood of any given enterprise are protected with entrenched immune systems that make it impossible to challenge the legacy business. Forging new business models requires an environment in which culture, priorities, and processes are malleable. We chose the colony metaphor deliberately to evoke the independence that's essential to innovation. The alternatives—skunkworks, intrapreneurship programs, innovation labs, startup partnerships—are demonstrably ineffective at producing new high-growth businesses. Their biggest weakness is lack of autonomy.

Free from the need to fulfill enterprise priorities, an innovation colony can move quickly to learn what customers want, build it, and reach markets ahead of competitors. It can develop products that compete directly with the corporation's existing lines of business and attract entrepreneurial talent that wouldn't consider working for a large company. It's positioned to do whatever it needs to do in pursuit of growth.

## Objection: Enterprises Don't Need an Innovation Colony, They Need an Innovative Culture

Enterprise culture minimizes risk. Startup culture embraces risk. It's so tempting for executives to believe that their corporations can be led to take greater risks and their employees inspired to place big bets in the face of uncertainty. But company culture isn't so malleable. It arises from the structures and processes that enable the company to do what it does, and that it has been doing for years. Culture can't be changed in isolation. That kind of change requires altering the components that make the company what it is—in which case it would no longer be the same company.

Instead of trying to change company culture, you need to create a new and different kind of organization that provides fertile ground for the culture you want to grow. Think of an innovation colony as an island far away from the enterprise "mainland" in which taking daring risks is the norm, employees sink or swim on their own initiative, and they're amply rewarded when their bets pay off. The colonists think entrepreneurially on a daily basis, not just during the rare moments when it's called for or when entrepreneurship accords well with company budgets or politics. Over time, an ability to create new, disruptive businesses becomes their core competency.

## Objection: Sharing Upside to Employees Is Complicated, Costly, or Unnecessary

To many enterprise executives, the notion of sharing equity is counterintuitive. They're accustomed to creating value by paying salaries or stock in the corporation. They may feel as though the enterprise's support—cash, marketing muscle, distribution network, technology portfolio—is more valuable than their employees' product-development efforts. And they may have a hard time empathizing with the entrepreneurial urge. After all, in most cases they've dedicated their career to climbing the corporate ladder, not building their own company.

What those executives are missing is the extraordinary motivational power of ownership. Speaking with Instagram cofounder Kevin Systrom on his TechCrunch video show, *Founder Stories* host Chris Dixon made an astute observation: "Ownership is a critical part of why you stay up all night and why you think about it all day, every day. I don't know if stock options in Microsoft can ever feel like ownership." In other words, entrepreneurs will give their all if they have the right incentive, and their all is necessary to bring their ideas to product/market fit. They need to own the startups they're working on, and if they can't do it within the enterprise, the most determined of them will strike out on their own. That's partly about the slim chance of beating the system by hitting it big. But it's also about pride and legacy: Entrepreneurs want to leave new empires when they're gone.

Sharing upside with employees doesn't have to be overly complicated or generous. Flip the usual viewpoint: Trading equity for salary actually mitigates the enterprise's risk. It usually cuts salaries by 50 percent, enabling the company to hire a larger innovation staff. More people means better diversification of a portfolio among a large number of investments. If you're lucky enough to score a hit, but walk away feeling as though you gave away too much equity, try giving away less next time and see how that goes. The build, measure, learn cycle applies at almost all levels of the business, and this is one of them.

### Objection: Lean Startup Techniques Can't Generate Complicated Products

Many people are under the misconception that lean startup is for building toys, not *serious products*. Enterprise executives are accustomed to knowing best. Due to generational issues, they may have experience with *waterfall* delivery methods. These time-proven models are fine ways to build things when you know exactly what you want to make and you don't change your mind. They're also great for building stuff that nobody wants or needs.

We think that one of the roots of this misconception is that the initial output of lean startup-style experimentation and iteration is a scaled-down minimum viable product (MVP). If that's all you ever get out of lean startup, then the objection starts to make sense. But in reality, that minimum output is just the beginning, not the end, of a sustainable business. An MVP ensures that you build the right product for your customers, and that initial step can serve as the core for building a more extensive offering that scales efficiently to a larger market.

There's no reason why a minimum viable product's scope can't grow along with the development team's ambition. Look at IMVU, the company founded by Eric Ries, creator of Lean Startup. It's a large-scale virtual world with lots of technology under the hood. What began as a minimum viable product evolved steadily over the years into an elaborate and extensive infrastructure for exploration, social interactions, and play. All while continuously applying and evolving the lean startup application of the build-measure-learn cycle.

Done right, we know that the lean startup method gets even large, complex products to market faster and cheaper than any other approach. Its greatest benefit, from an enterprise perspective, is avoiding catastrophic product failures. Nothing can damage an executive's career like a big failed product launch, and nothing is more damaging to staff morale than wasting resources on an effort that many thought didn't make sense to begin with. By ensuring that every feature serves customer needs, the lean startup method guides teams toward success whether the final product is simple and small or complex and sprawling.

## Objection: Why Incubate or Acquire Early When You Can Buy a Proven Startup?

Corporate development departments are ever on the lookout for companies to acquire. And it's not just tech giants like Microsoft, Google, and Facebook doing the buying. Huge corporations in agriculture, automobile, health, financial services, and even retail are out hunting for talent in Silicon Valley and beyond.

They look for ventures whose activities are synergistic with the enterprise's established lines of business. And that means startups that are in gear and moving forward. It makes intuitive sense that the enterprise can use its considerable resources to help the acquisition grow.

However, this strategy comes with its own risks. There's bound to be limited upside in later-stage acquisition, which significantly narrows your potential gains. Acquiring a company that has momentum means paying a high price and potentially giving the founders a huge payday that lets them kick back and relax (on their new yacht). Plus, if you think about it, the founders who are most willing to sell their companies will be those who are least confident in their ability to grow beyond the value you offer up.

And then there's the challenge of integrating the startup with the culture of a large enterprise. Acquiring early minimizes or sidesteps these hazards. You get a bargain on a vigorous young company that's on the verge of breaking new, lucrative ground.

Note that we're not saying that acquiring early replaces usual *corp dev* acquisitions. We see it as a separate activity that carries high risk, but promises much higher rewards. The innovation colony's acquisitions aren't intended to create synergies for existing business lines, but to foster disruptive innovations that let the enterprise remain healthy over the long run.

### Objection: Real Men Don't Pivot

As with many elements of the lean startup philosophy, the concept of the pivot provokes in some observers a macho posture that amounts to, "pivots are for weaklings."

Funny, but true story: In early 2013 the two of us flew out to Silicon Valley for an in-person interview with Y Combinator for acceptance into their prestigious accelerator program. During our conversation, one of the partners exclaimed, "Oh gawd, if we let you guys in here we're going to have to hear the word 'pivot' all the time!"

His eyes rolled so far back in his head we worried he might have a seizure! But seriously, there's a tendency out there, especially among the privileged set, to view pivoting as indecisive and undisciplined. That mind-set can be especially strong in enterprises that have prospered by staying the course for decades. Even prominent people in the startup community, such as Techstars NYC's David Tisch and Brooklyn Bridge Ventures' Charlie O'Donnell, have publicly expressed skepticism about the value of pivoting.

The thing is, markets in which "staying the course" is a winning strategy are becoming fewer by the year. Given the speed of technological development and the unpredictability of market shifts, a willingness to pivot is a prerequisite for innovation. Pivoting based on sound metrics modeling doesn't betray a lack of commitment. It's an adjustment to real-world conditions based on evidence. Moreover, entrepreneurs who are incentivized by equity in their own startups will take great care to pivot only when an invalid hypothesis has run its course.

For the enterprise, pivoting means higher returns, faster, and at lower cost. Some members of the innovation team will pivot too early, too frequently, or the wrong way—we see that all the time among our corporate clients. But we also see that they learn from experience and get better over time. As they figure it out, the innovation colony as a whole benefits.

## Building Innovation Empires

For enterprises that manage to get past their skepticism and embrace the innovation colony concept wholeheartedly, a question arises: Why stop at one? Did the British Empire have just one colony?

An innovation colony must be driven by a distinctive innovation thesis to be effective, but there's no reason why an enterprise must settle on just a single line of entrepreneurial enquiry. Colonists who are passionate about, say, tablet apps may be housed in a mobile-focused colony while those who are inspired by hardware may occupy another and those who are driven to pursue opportunities in services occupy yet another. Or different colonies may address specific regional markets. We don't see a reason why the ambitious executive wouldn't strive to build an *innovation empire*.

We don't see a practical limit on this line of thinking. The more innovation colonies an enterprise has, the more innovative and entrepreneurial expertise it accumulates, and the more it benefits from exchanges of information and personnel among colonies.

Famous venture capitalist Ron Conway once said, "There's a billion-dollar company created every three months." Now, it is every two months. Any enterprise hoping to claim that kind of opportunity would need to make the establishment of innovation colonies a core competency.

In time, innovation colonies could even replace conventional business units. Today's business units may be cash cows, but their life expectancy becomes shorter every year. Existing lines of business must renew themselves continuously or risk disruption in an ever broader range of industries. They may have greater longevity as innovation colonies with tightly formulated innovation theses. Just as innovation colonies don't hesitate to spin out companies that compete with the enterprise's core businesses, they shouldn't waver over opportunities that compete with companies they've already spun out. Their job is to innovate within their purview and reap the rewards.

## The End of Entrepreneurship

Innovative entrepreneurship has reached an inflection point. Until recently it was an art, chiefly available to those with talent, means, or the good fortune to apprentice themselves to masters. Increasingly, though, we think it's becoming a science, especially with anything involving software. (And remember, "software is eating the world.")

Web-hosting services, high-level programming languages, open-source software, and pervasive social media provide an infrastructure that makes product development faster, cheaper, and easier than ever before. And the formulation of lean startup methods has made it possible to consistently build things that customers will buy. The necessary skills are being taught in business schools, publicized by accelerators, and proliferated by organizations like our own Lean Startup Machine. These developments have transformed entrepreneurship from a shot in the dark into a viable career choice.

So now what? We think that innovation colonies are the next link in the chain. As things stand, enterprises have no real advantage over startups; in fact, they have a ton of disadvantages. But as they implement lean startup practices, establish innovation colonies, and perfect the management disciplines involved, they have the opportunity to overshadow independent entrepreneurs. They can collect and organize the resources needed to launch new companies, removing the coordination costs of starting new businesses and creating a frictionless environment for disruptive innovation. There will be more friction to building a new company on your own than building it within an enterprise innovation colony.

The ascendency of enterprises as innovators doesn't mean that Silicon Valley will dry up and blow away, but it will face a new, formidable rival: the lean enterprise.

The advantages of lean enterprises are obvious based on capital resources alone. Total U.S. venture investments amounted to $29.4 billion in 2013, according to the National Venture Capital Association. In contrast, the top five cash-rich U.S. corporations, Apple, Microsoft, Google, Pfizer, and Cisco, held $347 billion in 2012. These companies could out-innovate Sand Hill Road simply by putting 10 percent of their war chest into innovation colonies. Corporations that seize the initiative to innovate face an open field of untapped opportunity.

As enterprises flex their entrepreneurial muscles, they will have a dramatic impact on the way we think about entrepreneurship. Think about how today's most successful entrepreneurs are revered as rock stars, to be seen at parties and political fundraisers, interviewed on talk shows, and lionized in Hollywood movies. The Internet era has spawned larger-than-life characters as much as it has delivered unexpected new tools and toys. Consider Steve Jobs, an icon of audacity, imagination, and persistence or Mark Zuckerberg, an emblem of youthful energy and intelligent rebellion. How many new entrepreneurs have those guys inspired!

But we think that ultimately the institutionalization of entrepreneurship will drain the romance out of entrepreneurial accomplishments until they become a matter of professional competence rather than heroic triumph against all odds.

## The Enterprise Innovation Era

The passing of entrepreneurship as an object of romance will signal the end of an era of dramatic, exciting change in business and society alike.

Not everyone will welcome the new age, and even we have mixed feelings when we envision it! Just as online dating is baffling, even offensive in the eyes of our parents' generation, the rise of enterprise-driven innovation will upset those who value rugged individualism over systematic efficiency.

The coming innovation empires will form vast expanses of creative exploration and business acumen on a scale never seen before. Given immense resources, savvy management, and ever more refined techniques for reaching product/market fit, innovation colonies probe real problems and will develop novel solutions at an unparalleled rate. Their organizational structure will reflect the realities of the networked market, bringing small teams to bear on unpredictable market shifts with the greatest possible speed to win emerging markets. Innovation colonies will incubate, acquire, and invest as needed to stake their claim on the most potent technologies and trends ahead of the pack. Their autonomous management will keep their usual corporate instincts for self-protection and self-promotion in check. The managing directors, liberated from fealty to the enterprise budget, will navigate the market for the colony's wares with a free hand. The colonists, beneficiaries of a growing portfolio of projects painstakingly tailored to the needs of real-world customers, will move their projects forward with singular ingenuity and focus.

It's an exciting time. We are witnessing a new dawn of enterprise innovation. We are awakening to a richer world for customers of all kinds. We are ever faster delivering solutions to people's most pressing problems, as well as satisfaction of their fleeting whims. We are embracing innovation on a scale and at a pace never before seen. Welcome to the era of the lean enterprise.

# About the Authors

Trevor Owens met **Obie Fernandez** on a cold winter weekend in Chicago. The latter cheekily strolled into one of the first Lean Startup Machine (LSM) workshops without even bothering to register. They established a quick friendship and Obie became an advisor to Trevor's fledgling startup a few months later. The two even became roommates for awhile, when Obie spent the first half of 2011 living in NYC. Over the course of 2011 and 2012, with Obie's help, Trevor drove LSM to tremendous worldwide growth, training over 25 thousand students around the world to apply Lean Startup methods to their own startup ambitions. In January 2013, Obie formally joined LSM as Co-Founder and CTO, to help propel the firm to new heights. They subsequently were accepted to the prestigious Techstars accelerator program and raised $1.5M in venture capital funding.

**Trevor** is an entrepreneur and thought leader on Lean Startup methodologies. He's the Founder & CEO of Lean Startup Machine, an innovation education company that has helped thousands of individuals at organizations including Google, Salesforce, News Corp, Intuit, and others, start hundreds of new businesses on five continents. He is active in the community as a coach for the White House's Innovation Fellows program and as a featured guest speaker at Princeton & Columbia University.

**Obie** is a widely recognized technology leader and frequent speaker at industry events. He is Addison Wesley's Series Editor for the best-selling Professional Ruby Series and a serial entrepreneur. Prior to founding LSM and his iconic web agency, Hashrocket, Obie spent years as a senior consultant at ThoughtWorks, specializing in complex custom enterprise software projects. He has been hacking computers since he got his first Commodore VIC-20 in the eighties, and found himself in the right place and time as a programmer on some of the first Java enterprise projects of the mid-nineties.

# Index